Founded in 1949, the **Council of Europe** is an intergovernmental organisation of thirty-nine member states.[1] Among its aims are: protecting and strengthening pluralist democracy and human rights, promoting the emergence of a genuine European cultural identity, seeking solutions to the problems facing society (the position of minorities, xenophobia and intolerance, environmental protection, bioethics, Aids, drugs, etc.), developing a political partnership with the new democracies of central and eastern Europe, and helping these same countries with their political, legislative and constitutional reforms.

The *Committee of Ministers* is the Council's decision-making body, made up of the foreign ministers of the thirty-nine member states or their permanent representatives. The consultative organ is the *Parliamentary Assembly* whose members are appointed by national parliaments. The *Congress of Local and Regional Authorities of Europe* is a consultative body representing local communities and regions.

The **Parliamentary Assembly** of the Council of Europe was the first European assembly to be created in the history of the continent. With delegations from thirty-nine national parliaments it is still the largest European assembly. The Assembly, which determines its own agenda, deals with current affairs and topical themes affecting society and international policy. It meets four times a year in the debating chamber of the *Palais de l'Europe* in plenary session open to the public. Its work has an important influence in determining the activities of the Committee of Ministers. Matters discussed by the

---

1. Member states of the Council of Europe (at 1 March 1996): Albania, Andorra, Austria, Belgium, Bulgaria, Czech Republic, Cyprus, Denmark, Estonia, Finland, the former Yugoslav Republic of Macedonia, France, Germany, Greece, Hungary, Iceland, Ireland, Italy, Latvia, Liechtenstein, Lithuania, Luxembourg, Malta, Moldova, Netherlands, Norway, Poland, Portugal, Romania, Russian Federation, San Marino, Slovak Republic, Slovenia, Spain, Sweden, Switzerland, Turkey, Ukraine, United Kingdom.

Parliamentary Assembly are also reported back by representatives to their national parliaments, and thus have an influence on governments.

The child as citizen is based on the reports and opinions given by the committees of the Parliamentary Assembly of the Council of Europe.

The following documents were used in the compilation of this book:
Doc. 6142 (Mrs Ekman), Doc. 6150 (Mr Bowden), Doc. 7270 (Mrs Jaani), Doc. 7436 (Mr Cox), Doc. 7473 (Mrs Err).

This book does not include the work undertaken by the Steering Committee on Social Policy and the European Committee on Legal Co-operation within the context of the Council of Europe's Inter-governmental Work Programme.

Your children are not your children.
They are the sons and daughters of life's longing for itself.
They came through you but not from you,
And though they are with you yet they belong not to you.

Kahlil Gibran, *The Prophet*

Contents

Foreword

by Carol Bellamy[1]

There are three pieces of good news for Europe's 200 million children: all but one of the member states of the Council of Europe have ratified the United Nations Convention on the Rights of the Child; the Council of Europe – the continent's most geographically encompassing organisation and its most respected human rights institution – has now taken the basic tenets of this convention and developed a European Strategy for Children; and the Council of Europe has opened for signature a European Convention on the Exercise of Children's Rights.

The European Strategy for Children, adopted on 24 January 1996 by the Parliamentary Assembly of the Council of Europe, is an exemplary document, and one that merits careful study by other regions and countries equally determined to make the transition from commitment to action.

When the convention on children's rights was first drafted during the eighties, no one imagined that just a few years later it would become the most widely-ratified human rights instrument in history: as of mid-March 1996, 187 states are parties to the convention. Children's rights are now universal law.

When it was first adopted on 20 November 1989, many people in the developed world thought of the convention as an instrument

---

1. Executive director of Unicef, Geneva.

9

intended mainly for other countries, those still striving to achieve the "basics" of education, health care, nutrition, water and sanitation – all now taken for granted in the industrialised world. There was a temptation to think that children in their own countries were fine, and that only minor changes would be required as a result of ratifying the convention.

However, the United Nations Committee on the Rights of the Child, in its concluding observations after reviewing initial states party reports, found that there are children in every country in the world whose rights are not being fully met. There are children living in impoverished families, or without families; children who belong to minority groups, children suffering the effects of financial cutbacks, children who are refugees or who are seeking asylum – and children who are in other ways marginalised or who do not enjoy the full range of economic, social and cultural, civil and political rights as laid down in the fifty-four articles of the convention.

Even where the rights of basic survival and development may be ensured, further progress must be made in the area of child protection. Child neglect, abuse and exploitation remain problems in all countries. So, too, must children's rights to participation be more widely respected and supported, for when children have a say in decisions affecting their lives – "in a manner consistent with the evolving capacities of the child" – they grow into more active and conscientious citizens of more democratic societies. Children's voices need to be heard and their opinions taken into account.

This requires a new vision of the child – not as a mini-adult or as a minor, but rather as a developing human being, endowed with all rights from the beginning, and growing to contribute to his or her society. The convention considers the child a person, and children's essential needs as rights which the adult world – individuals, families, communities and governments – are obligated to respect and fulfil.

The European Strategy for Children calls on all member states: to implement children's rights as a matter of political priority; to afford children first call on all resources, including budgetary resources; to follow a multidisciplinary approach at all levels, from the ministerial governmental level to the local administration, in order to approach each child as a whole human being; to evaluate every new law with the help of a child impact statement; and to appoint an ombudsperson for children.

In addition, the strategy also calls for a permanent multidisciplinary intergovernmental structure involving Unicef, the United Nations Committee on the Rights of the Child, the European Parliament, non-governmental organisations and children themselves. This structure is to act as a beacon of hope and a permanent spotlight. It will continue the monitoring of progress and development of new policy, as required, to fully satisfy the requirements of the convention.

Just as the Council of Europe rose from the ashes of the second world war as a harbinger of democracy, the rule of law and human rights, so the European Strategy for Children grew from the suffering of the children of the former Yugoslavia. The impetus to draft such a strategy arose at a joint meeting of Unicef and the Council of Europe's Parliamentary Assembly, early in 1993, on the situation of women and children suffering in the worst post-second world war conflict in Europe.

Over 50 000 children have been the victims of conflict in the former Yugoslavia. I sincerely hope that all member states and peoples of Europe will join forces to implement the recommendations of the European Strategy for Children. I hope that the political will expressed in this strategy may endure as a monument to the memory of those children. And I also hope that its full implementation will contribute, in perhaps small but still significant ways, to preventing the outbreak of future conflicts.

I also believe the convention can transcend borders as it calls on richer nations to assist poorer ones in meeting the needs and ensuring the rights of all children. With its long and proud tradition of human rights, Europe can – and, I believe, must – play a major role in helping to advance the rights of children everywhere.

A poet once summed it up like this: "A child – every child – is another chance to get it right". The European Strategy for Children can help all of us "get it right". Unicef is proud to accompany Europe in the great cause of securing the rights of children everywhere.

Introduction

Society's attitudes towards children have undergone major changes throughout this century. The international community has largely acknowledged that children are vulnerable and need special care and protection from parents and society. It was, however, only recently that children were recognised as legal subjects and bearers of rights.

The fundamental rights of the child have been recognised nearly everywhere, at least in theory. The United Nations Convention on the Rights of the Child,[1] is the legal reference instrument and the framework for action. This convention, adopted in 1989, and which is ratified by nearly all the member states of the Council of Europe, recognises the indivisibility of civil, political, social, economic and cultural rights. However, numerous reservations have been made.

Children's rights are also protected by the European Convention on Human Rights and the European Social Charter, both Council of Europe instruments, as well as by the recent European Convention on the Exercise of Children's Rights opened to signature in January 1996. The European Convention on Human Rights does not refer explicitly to children's rights but covers "everyone"; the Parliamentary Assembly of the Council of Europe has frequently called for specific protocols on children's rights (see its Opinion No. 186

---

1. As of 1 March 1996 187 states have ratified this convention.

on the draft European convention on the exercise of children's rights).

The European Social Charter covers children's rights, albeit not comprehensively. It contains two articles: Article 7 on the protection of children and young persons at work and Article 17 on mothers and young children. The draft revised charter will contain a more comprehensive provision on children.

But what has been achieved in terms of practical implementation? Additional action is necessary.

Europe is a rich and developed continent. Despite this, extreme poverty does not spare children and in all too many cases they are still far from being perceived and treated as human beings in their own right. In central and eastern Europe, it is they who are paying the heaviest price for the transition to the market economy and democracy: large numbers are finding themselves the defenceless victims of privatisation and the accompanying economic constraints, with dramatic consequences in terms of falling health standards, sharp drops in educational provisions and a rising number of children being abandoned. The armed conflict in the former Yugoslavia has revealed the deficiencies in the protection of the civilian population and, in particular, children.

As the meeting place for dialogue between western European countries and the new democracies of central and eastern Europe, the Council of Europe is the ideal forum for defining the principles and content of a Europe-wide strategy, taking account of the different situations throughout the continent and with reference to the United Nations Convention on Children's Rights.

Such a strategy should inspire action and policies at international and national levels and guide the efforts of all those who actively support children's causes. It should set out a catalogue of common aims for improving the conditions in which children live and trigger debate at national and European level so that we can find out more about the situation of children and the extent to which the various international commitments already entered into are applied. Since problems differ from one country to another, it will be left to each country to devise its own action plan.

Promoting the rights of children has been a long-standing concern of the international community and of the Council of Europe in particular. Admittedly, the work in this field is delicate and demands a careful approach, because it inevitably affects the private sphere of family life. Unlike traditional legal rights disputes where the individual is confronted with other individuals or the government, the children's rights debate is complicated by the question of parental rights and responsibilities. The efforts of law-makers have, therefore, been concentrated on finding the proper balance between the rights and responsibilities of parents, on the one hand, the rights of children, on the other hand, and the special obligation of the state to protect children.

A new vision of childhood

by Karl Eric Knutsson[1]

There is at the moment a promising momentum – politically and in the public opinion – with regard to child-related issues. To understand and strengthen this we need to articulate major perceptions that may influence our views and recommendations; the knowledge base on which we build our arguments; and the major rationale for proposing a strategy for children on a regional, European scale. If we do not do this it will be difficult to argue the need of such a strategy and to convince those who require convincing.

Knowledge base

My arguments assume a fundamental assimilation and integration of children and childhood – theoretically, ethically and practically – in other forms and on all levels of human reality. To understand the implications of this view we have to assemble knowledge gained from studies on psycho-motor forms of child development and in the fields of economic development and the improvement of the human condition.

Urie Bronfenbrenner has made proposals which link these two perspectives. They constitute, to paraphrase Amartya Sen's words, a

---

1. Karl Eric Knutsson is head of research at the International Child Development Centre, Unicef, Florence. This contribution was written at the request of the Social, Health and Family Affairs Committee of the Parliamentary Assembly of the Council of Europe.

"moral minimum" for child-related development. "The effective functioning of child-rearing processes in the family and other child settings requires public policies and practices that provide place, time, stability, status, recognition, belief systems, customs and actions in support of child-rearing activities not only on the part of parents, care givers, teachers and other professional personnel, but also relatives, friends, neighbours, co-workers, communities, and major economic, social and political institutions of society as a whole."[1]

To create such conditions and to achieve such goals means that individual and community values as well as public policies must be reoriented towards a genuine integration of children and childhood in theory and in practice. This requires fundamental changes in our efforts to analyse child-related development. We have to abandon our hopes that development will happen through some kind of linear approach. Instead we have to outline what kind of society we want and what it takes to get there. Planning will be an exercise in working backwards from such basic principles and identifying what is needed to put them in place.

Perceptions of children

The most common perception of children is a charitable one, an attitude which mainly draws strength from a feeling of responsibility for the suffering child. When combined, as was the case in the last centure, with the perception of the "innocent and sacred" child, the basis was laid for some of the strongest tenets in both national and international concern for children.

---

1. U. Bronfenbrenner, "Discovering what families do", pp 27-38 in Blankenhoorn, Bayne and Ehlshtain, eds: *Rebuilding the nests:a new commitment to the American family*. Milwaukee, WI. Family Service America, p.37.

Another long-held perception was the emergency-humanitarian approach to child suffering. It had and has as its dominant goal the saving of children's lives and their protection from hunger, disease and other immediate sufferings.

A third concern for children which emerged, adopted a developmental approach. It was based on a combination of rationales of which the most prominent were that children ought to be allowed to grow to their full potential both physically and intellectually. In this it had elements of an early child development and human rights approach. However, behind these there were also interests that children thereby would become, as adults, more mature, useful and "effective" citizens.

A fourth cluster of perceptions has become increasingly prominent over the last decades. It is best summarised by the Unicef term: child survival and development. It represents a combination of emergency and developmental approaches. It proposes that available technologies and other means of development should be put to maximum use especially for the many who live their lives in the "silent" emergencies caused by poverty, disease and a hazardous and brutal environment. It also emphasises the need to use a cost-effectiveness calculus to decide on 'do-able' goals and strategies which can be promoted while recognising constraints in financial and other resources.

In all these different perceptions there is a strong tendency to see the child in isolation. When this view is combined with any of the four over-arching clusters identified above it gives rise to goals and strategies which are very different from those which emphasise the embeddedness of children and childhood in society.

Other variations in perceptions are linked to norms in societies which allocate responsibilities for children differently. These responsibilities are generally subdivided on the basis of gender and depending on the phase of childhood that the child belongs to. In addition there are different views on how society operates or ought to operate, especially in terms of the organisation of the state. Such views will influence how policies for children are managed. This is a major divide in the choice of strategies and has created important variations in approaches.

Children and society: recognising the child as a citizen

In his important programmatic statement "children as a social phenomenon", Quortrup asks "can society carry any responsibility for children?" There are three major arguments for such a responsibility. The first one is a moral argument ensuring that children are provided for in accordance with a basic standard, or that the standard of life for a family with children be on a par with that of a couple without children.[1]

There is also the "end-result" argument. It is based on the fact – still to be accepted in many circles – that children are making crucial contributions to the construction of society and to its biological, organisational and cultural reproduction. Because of this they have a legitimate and undisputable claim on relevant and adequate resources within all the different dimensions of social and cultural life.

Society has a number of interests in children – if not in children while they are children, then at least in children as the next generation. This interest translates into corresponding responsibilities for children. Society ought also to take an interest in children while they are children not merely for emotional, charity or ethical reasons. After all they are members of one of society's major groups

---

1. Quortrup, *Children as a Social Phenomenon*, 1993, page 17.

of citizens. If all other reasons are disregarded this in itself constitutes a fundamental obligation on the part of society.

There is an increasing need – not least in industrial and post industrial societies where new perceptions of children as pets, expensive luxuries or as sources of nuisance are spreading – to stress the fact that childhood is an integral part of society and its division of labour. This can be called the utilitarian argument for the incorporation of children and childhood at the heart of social, economic and political considerations. This should not be interpreted as a plea for the legitimisation of child labour in the conventional sense. It is an argument for the recognition of school-labour as an intrinsic part of the division of labour which cannot be separated from labour in society at large.

Perception of children and their rights

The notion of child development – nationally and internationally – basically started as a children's rights movement even if early articulations of such rights were tentative and vague. The efforts to include concern for children in mainstream development planning, which began in earnest in the 1960's, can actually be seen as efforts to use developmental arguments and strategies to achieve fundamental rights for children. The same assessment is valid for later periods when strategies sometimes became heavily technology-driven. Regardless of other variations, there has always been a qualitative difference between movements to better the situation for children and mainstream economic development.

The declaration of the World Summit for Children and the United Nations Convention on the Rights of the Child contain important proposals for a theory of development incorporating children. In the convention these can be subdivided into four major clusters: the first contains goals and outlines some strategic elements

21

required for the survival of children. It covers such major elements as health, food, and other basic needs.

The second deals with the promotion and strengthening of a caring environment and points to the need of support for the main providers of care such as women/mothers in general and women in the various phases of the perinatal process in particular.

The third cluster can be described as the construction, maintenance and strengthening of a nurturing environment. It ranges from such broader issues as the obligation of the state to an improved allocation of critical resources for children in terms of finances, expertise, policies and administrative arrangements. It calls for universalisation of relevant basic education for all with special efforts to redress gender distortions. It identifies priorities and obligations for international aid and development organisations and supports more equitable opportunities for poor countries in the organisation of international trade. It stipulates efforts aiming towards poverty reduction and involvement of local communities. Emphasis is also laid on improvement of administration and management.

The fourth cluster concerns the need to create and enforce a protective environment and deals with the unconscionable suffering of children in war and social and political conflicts, child abuse and child exploitation – sexually and as labour – abandonment and other difficult circumstances damaging children especially in minority situations and in physically and socially degraded living conditions.

The intergenerational perspective

To these arguments in favour of a comprehensive strategy for children should be added a couple of others. One could be called the limited field argument. It represents views that have been widely held during various phases of human history and in many cultural traditions but which were weakened in recent ideologies of political and economic expansion and by the accompanying industrialisation which became their technological vehicle. At present, even the exploitative society is finally realising that we are facing a dramatically changed situation compared to the heyday of growth euphoria. Two major factors are beginning to strengthen the basis for this argument. One is the limit of physical resources and their appalling waste.

Another major factor is that, effective as political, economic and cultural globalisation have been over the last centuries from the point of view of the developed countries, the globe itself is increasingly setting boundaries for an "open system" version of globalisation. Increasingly the planet itself is becoming the maximum operating field for major processes and strategies. This is changing the rules of the game from an "open systems" approach with all its possibilities for compensation of deficiencies or needs in the developed countries through continued expansion. Instead the situation is turning both theoretically and practically into a "closed systems" situation where it is increasingly difficult to pass on costs from the dominant countries to the dominated. Instead they are increasingly passed on to future generations. This requires that we must radically redefine the space/time dimensions within which efforts to better the human condition and thereby the conditions of children are considered, planned and implemented. Generally these concerns are restricted to the periods of political interest in the subject by those in power at the time and are limited by the availability of financial resources, arbitrarily chosen durations of a project or other such external critera.

This must be substituted by a "process" approach which recognises the intergenerational nature of major child-related problems and similar long-term responsibilities of adult society.

The process as a goal: towards a culture of partnership

There are signs, in both poor and rich countries, that quality of life is being eroded due to sheer neglect: families do not hold together, schools do not teach, politics invite cynicism, companies exploit, environments pollute, communities are disappearing. This is the social environment over which governments are called upon to preside and which explains why an increasing number of citizens, especially children and women, are neglected, abused, handicapped or discriminated against.

These vicious circles can, and must, be broken. The future can be different, but only if positive links are fostered towards common goals for the betterment of the conditions for the excluded.

These goals must comprise links between the government and the community in a political process and links between various disciplines and areas of human endeavour, at a professional level. These two sets of links should not be difficult to establish, but experience suggests that there are serious obstacles.

As part of the institutional decline, the distance between the governments and communities has increased over time. Governments have grown larger and more impersonal. And the community has been ground small between a non-participatory industrial culture and eroding natural life-support systems.

In conjunction with this same unrestrained process, various specialties have developed, often without a common language of interdisciplinary communication. As a result, development has often lost its human focus, leaving the majority in the outer court. The basic human right to live, grow and to be recognised and respected has become a casualty, not an achievement.

To plead for a change in emphasis is not to argue for neglect of humanitarian welfare, physical infrastructure nor growth in material terms, but only to correct the serious distortions that have followed in the wake of the institutional decline.

A return not only to the roots of the problems but also to the level where the action is, is called for – namely the small community in the rural area, the tribal village, the urban slum. Today, that community is diminished, fragmented, unorganised, not fully informed, and active far below the required level. At national and international levels, there are many fora for discussion and supportive action. However necessary, these can never be a substitute for solidarity and group action at community level, supported by informed and committed civil servants from the various arms and levels of government working effectively together. The absence of this foundation at the level where things have to happen, explains the tardiness of progress towards realising human goals. This is one strong reason why we have to remember that the way in which we choose to achieve social – and thereby child-related goals – is not simply a choice of strategy or tactic. It is a goal in itself.

Defining children's rights

When talking about the rights of children people generally mean to say that children are in need of protection and that they have a right to protection. This perspective means looking at the way children are protected and the way in which their protection may be improved at national or international level and studying the corresponding obligations of parents, teachers and other educators as well as those of society and the public authorities. Much has been done and much remains to be done here.[1]

Although parents, teachers and other adults, as a rule, will have the interest of children in mind, there may be cases in which there is a conflict of interests. Small conflicts are, of course, a daily phenomenon in human relations and, normally, they are solved in an atmosphere of mutual understanding and confidence. Thus the adult may take due account of the child's wishes, avoiding imposing his will unless he feels it is called for. The child, on the other hand, will recognise the adult's authority, experience and good faith, and accept his decisions. When there is a real conflict which

---

1. See for instance Recommendation 1071 (1988) on child welfare – Providing institutional care for infants and children; Doc. 5854, report of the Social, Health and Family Affairs Committee (rapporteur: Mr Oehler) and also Recommendation 874 (1979) on a European charter on the rights of the child; Doc. 4376, report of the Social, Health and Family Affairs Committee. The protection of children is also the guiding principle of the questionnaire which was prepared recently for the Conference of European Ministers for Family Affairs (Autumn 1989) and which bears the title "Methods of child upbringing in Europe today and the role of family services".

cannot be solved smoothly young children will generally have to give in. But when they grow up their judgment matures and the interests at stake may increase. Then there may be situations in which their rights and their wishes should – and quite often do – prevail over those of the opposing adults. There is a factual situation here which frequently constitutes a grey area from a legal point of view.

The distinction between the rights of children and their protection is not always that important. The question at stake is whether a young person would need intervention and assistance or not when asserting the rights granted to him.

The position of the child in court

Do children have the right to institute legal proceedings and are there, in their member state, special judges to determine children's civil rights and obligations or any criminal charge against them.

In Austria, Belgium, the Federal Republic of Germany, Luxembourg, Netherlands, Norway, Spain, Turkey and other member states, children have no right of their own to institute legal proceedings but must be represented by the person who exercises parental authority. In Ireland, procedures are normally done on behalf of the child by a parent or guardian *ad litem*, in the United Kingdom by an adult "next friend". In Norway, a young person may act independently from the age of 16, in Denmark and Sweden, in certain circumstances, such as assault and battery in Denmark. In France and Luxembourg, a minor may institute proceedings himself if he wants to complain about his family. In the Netherlands, the Council for Child Protection can, in certain cases, represent the child against the parents.

Swiss legislation is very elaborate on this point. As a general rule in Switzerland a child has no right to institute legal proceedings but exceptions are allowed when the child has sufficient discretion and in matters which concern him or her directly and personally.

When a child in one of the Council of Europe's member states is assumed to have reached the age of discretion in which he can be held liable for criminal acts, he may normally be brought before a special juvenile court. In the Federal Republic of Germany there are special juvenile courts for those from 14 to 18 years of age, in Spain for young persons under 16, in the United Kingdom for those under 17. The juvenile courts in the United Kingdom are, however, merely a special type of magistrates' court, and a similar situation exists in the Netherlands where every court has its own juvenile judge not only to judge penal matters but also such cases as guardianship and adoption. There are special courts to deal with family matters in Vienna, Graz and Linz but elsewhere in Austria the ordinary courts are competent.

In the Scandinavian countries and in Turkey, there are no special juvenile courts for criminal or civil matters, which are handled by the ordinary courts, but part of their work may have been taken over by the children's ombudsman (Norway). As well as the right to take part in court proceedings, the right of children to receive legal assistance from the person of their choice must be considered. The existence of a special ombudsman for children, such as in Norway, or in Sweden, is a much more flexible and accessible method of appeal than the courts. Such an ombudsman for children may counsel them and inform them on their rights, intervene and, if possible, take legal action on their behalf. In Sweden there is a private organisation, called *Rädda Barnen* (Save the Children) which assumes similar tasks to the Norwegian children's ombudsman. It is financed by the contributions of numerous private persons. Another Swedish organisation called *Bris* gives counsel to children over the telephone. Such a telephone service for children has proved to be very successful and useful in other countries, for example Italy.

Right to freedom of religion

In France and Luxembourg, children have, in principle, the right to freedom of religion but this provision is quite meaningless when they have not the right to practise freely the religion of their choice.[1] Quite often freedom of religion for children is subject to the general rules on the decision-making powers of children, that is to say that it is normally subject to parental authority (Netherlands, Spain, United Kingdom, etc). Parents are therefore able, in these countries, to force their children to attend specific church services and refuse them authorisation to go to others. This is not possible in Belgium where the constitution provides, in its Article 15, that "no person may be constrained to assist in any way in the acts and ceremonies of any form of worship, nor to observe its days of rest". A similar provision exists in the Constitution of Turkey (Article 24).

In Denmark, a child is not entitled to choose his or her own religion or to leave the religion in which he or she was registered at birth, but in Norway a child may do so at the age of 15 and in Switzerland at 16. It is only in Germany that there is a graduated system:

- at age 10 children must be heard by a court if their parents do not agree about their religion (for instance whether they should be educated at a Catholic or a Protestant school);

- at age 12 a child's religion cannot be changed without the authorisation of the child;

- at age 14 a child has the right to determine his or her religion and may adhere to the religious denomination or sect of his or her choice.

---

1. See Y. Alhalel-Esnault, *Les problèmes religieux de la famille en droit privé français*. Thesis, Rennes, 1975.

In Sweden, there is a state church and prevailing rules may therefore depart somewhat from those in other countries. Thus a child becomes a member of the Swedish state church if his or her mother or father is a member of the church (Sections 7 and 8 of the 1961 Act on Freedom of Religion). An application to join or leave the church on behalf of a young person who has reached the age of 15 may only be made with his or her consent (Sections 11 and 12).

Freedom of political thought

At which age may a child become a member of a political party? There is no limitation in law and a child of any age may become a member of a political party provided he or she fulfils the requirements of membership of that particular political party (this is the case in the Federal Republic of Germany, Belgium, Netherlands, Switzerland, United Kingdom). The replies of the Federal Republic of Germany and of the Netherlands even indicate these minimum age limits for the most important political parties in accordance with their articles of association[1] but in the Federal Republic of Germany parents may forbid membership of a political party until the child has reached majority age in accordance with the general provisions of the Civil Code.[2] This general rule is also stated for Luxembourg, Sweden and Spain and, no doubt, applies in many other countries as well. It is only in Denmark (16 years), Norway (15 years) and Turkey (21 years; Article 68 of the constitution) that the law *expressis verbis* states minimum ages for membership of a political party.

---

1. Federal Republic of Germany: 16 years for CDU and CSU (Christian Democrats), FDP (Liberals) and SPD (Socialists). No minimum provision for the Greens. In the Netherlands CDA (Christian Democrats) and VVD (Liberals) have no minimum age. For the Labour Party there is a minimum age of 16 and for D66 (left-wing Liberals) of 18 years.
2. Articles 1626 and 1631 BGB.

There are a great number of other fundamental rights which may be of importance to young persons such as freedom of movement (right to travel, right to obtain a passport), freedom of association, freedom of expression (may a young person establish a periodical of his own with his friends or produce radio broadcasts?), freedom of education (choice of school), freedom to work, freedom in the field of medicine (choice of physician, refusal to undergo a certain medical treatment or operation), not to mention such obvious human rights as the right to life, interdiction of inhuman or degrading treatment and interdiction of deprivation of liberty.

Although it is essential to recognise new rights for children, it is perhaps even more important to draw attention to the fact that children already have rights. More information on their rights must therefore be provided both to children and to adults.

The right to social protection – Children paying the price for transition[1]

Children living in Europe now constitute the first truly European generation. So they have to be educated not only in a European spirit, but also with a view to living in a more integrated Europe.

The situation of children in central and eastern European countries can be characterised as a transition crisis. In this area of Europe, children are the social segment that has paid by far the highest price for transition. Their situation has worsened at a far more rapid pace in comparison with the situation of other segments of our societies.

In the socialist system, the child occupies a special position in the social protection system. This position is explained not only in a

1. By Catalin Zamfir, Institute for the Quality of Life, Bucharest, 1995. Report drawn up at the request of the Social, Health and Family Affairs Committee.

moral and ideological sense (children are the future of the socialist society) but is also, and probably to a larger degree, the inevitable consequence of the economic policy: to combine the relatively high equal primary distribution with the redistribution according to needs.

A vigorous protection policy for children was a necessary accompaniment of low wages. The following mechanisms of child social protection were employed:

• High child allowance;

• Highly subsidised goods for children: the prices for such goods were significantly lower than for others;

• Free services: health, education, kindergarten, creche, leisure activities, including holidays.

In the 1980s the situation for children was adversely affected by the structural economic crisis in all socialist countries. They were affected by hidden unemployment and price increases, as incomes decreased in some countries, inflation eroded the standard of living.

Another problem was an increased scarcity of goods which in turn meant higher prices to buy them on the black market; and also the deterioration and sometimes disappearance of services. The institutions concerned with children's welfare deteriorated noticeably more rapidly than others.

In the first years of transition, the economies of these countries were most affected by two phenomena:

• The long term structural crisis of irrationally developed and poorly managed economies. Since 1980 almost all socialist economies entered a crisis period, with a fall in growth rate;

• The disaggregation of the socialist economies, both at an internal and external level.

The situation of children has been affected in a contradictory way. There were some positive consequences, but on the whole these were outweighed by the negative ones.

The positive consequences are that some services have been improved – but not a lot – in the field of education and health. Scarcity of goods has been eliminated and living conditions in the institutions have improved a lot.

The negative side has been the decrease in the standard of living of the vast majority of the population, for example the decrease of real wages; and the increase in unemployment. Families with more children are generally the same families with high unemployment and/or low wages. Economic inequality increased rapidly – families with children were losing considerably more than families without children.

Price liberalisation produced a higher increase in prices of goods for children (because these were particularly heavily subsidised) and child allowance has been eroded in real terms much more than the other incomes. Some services for children have improved their quality, but have been privatised, and thereby ceased to be freely available.

The deterioration of children's welfare cannot be explained simply by a decrease in incomes; there was also a rapid withdrawal by the state from its functions of social protection. Such a withdrawal could be explained by two reasons: on the one hand – economic crisis; on the other the ideological suspicion that a very high state involvement in social protection is a socialist concept. One factor was not taken into account: you cannot reduce social protection of children in conditions in which the incomes of the vast majority of the population, already very low, has further decreased.

Another factor has to be considered: in the competition for scarce state resources, children have not been an effective pressure group. So, the cuts in social expenditures have been very unequal, more with regards to children than to others.

Some indicators prove this massive worsening of the situation of children:

• the number of abandoned children, instead of decreasing as a result of legalisation of abortions (the case of Romania), remained approximately at the same, high level;

• school participation decreased, especially because of the poor, difficult, economic conditions, and high costs of school attendance;

• infant mortality and morbidity remain high.

Because of ongoing budget deficits, we can expect that pressure to cut expenditure will result in a further deterioration in children's welfare.

In conclusion, for eastern and central European countries it is absolutely necessary to reverse the present trend. The level of cash and in-kind transfer to families with children has to be a function of the level of poverty in that country. In cases of greater poverty, state support for children has to be higher.

Special mechanisms for promoting the interests of children have to be implemented, in order to counteract the low competitiveness of children for resources.

A minimum package of cash and transfers in kind for families with children (child allowance and/or tax benefits, free or subsidised services) should be proportionally related to the level of poverty.

Family planning should be promoted to avoid children being born when the parents do not desire them.

Problems relating to children's rights

Children's rights in the human rights context

- Right to freedom of thought, conscience and expression
  - At what age may a child become a member of a political party?
  - At what age may he or she become a member of a non-profit making association?
  - At what age may a child contest a family decision concerning him or her?

- Right to freedom
  - Is a child entitled to choose his or her own religion or to leave the religion in which he or she was registered at birth?
  - If so, at what age?
  - To what extent is a child entitled to participate or to refuse to participate in religious services and other religious activities?
  - At what age may a child join a religious organisation or sect?

- Right to freedom of movement
  - From what age may a child obtain an identity card?
  - From what age may he or she obtain a passport?
  - From what age may he or she freely and at any time cross the frontiers of the country of which he or she is a national or where he or she is ordinarily resident? Must he or she in all cases be accompanied?

The rights of children in the family context

- Adoption of children
  - From what age may a child agree or refuse to be adopted?
  - In what way does he or she participate in the adoption procedure?
  - Does a judicial authority have to take part in the procedure?
  - In what circumstances may the consent of a child's natural parents be dispensed with so that the child may be adopted swiftly or at least within a reasonable time?

- Marriage of children
  - May a child marry without obtaining the consent of his or her parents?
  - Is the intervention of a judicial authority (juvenile court, solicitor) necessary for a child to be able to marry?
- Recognition of a child
  - Is a child who becomes a parent entitled to recognise his or her new-born child?
  - In the case of divorce, may the child choose the parent her or she wishes to live with?
  - When a child is placed in an institution or a foster family, may he or she take part in the procedure followed and the choice made?
- Place of residence
  - May a child freely choose his or her place of residence?
  - May he or she leave the family home?
  - If so, at what age and on what conditions?
  - Is his or her freedom of movement subject to parental consent?

The rights of children in the judicial system

- Right to legal protection
  - What can a child do to defend him or herself against corporal punishment inflicted upon him or her (for example, by parents or teachers)?
  - May a child institute legal proceedings?
  - Is there an independent and impartial tribunal or judge established by law that will determine either a child's civil rights and obligations or any criminal charge against him or her?
  - Where there is a juvenile court established by law, what are its duties and powers?
  - May a child conduct his or her own defence or choose his or her own defence counsel?
  - Where a child cannot afford a defence lawyer, can he or she be assisted by a court-appointed lawyer free of charge where the interests of justice so require?

- May he or she either question defendants or prosecution witnesses him or herself or have them questioned?
- Can a child obtain the summonsing of a person cited in his or her application?
- Does a child have the right to have his or her point of view taken into account in the divorce or separation proceedings of his or her parents?

- Civil and criminal liability of children
  - From what age does a child become liable for damage caused to others?
  - Is a child personally liable by law or is his or her liability subordinate to his or her parents' liability?
  - Does your country's law draw a distinction between liability with fault and liability without fault in the case of children?
  - What does your country's criminal law provide for in respect of liability on the part of a child?
  - Is there a presumption of innocence in respect of children? How is this concept defined in your national legal system?
  - Are any special penalties laid down for children? If so, what are they? Describe any special penalties prescribed by your national legislation.
  - What guarantees regarding procedure and conditions of detention are afforded to a child offender or a child suspected of having committed a misdemeanour or a felony?

Children in the context of the school system

- Until what age is a child obliged to attend school?
- At what age does a child become free to choose his or her own school?
- At what age may a child accept or reject the academic or vocational choice made for him or her by his or her teachers or parents?
- Are information and advice centres available to give children guidance for their school or university courses?
- At what age may a child undertake vocational training?

- To what extent may children participate in the running of their schools?

Children in the social context

- Legal capacity
    - At what age does your country accord full legal majority and capacity? Please give details of full legal capacity and the conditions on which it may be exercised.
    - At what age may a child choose his or her nationality if he or she has more than one nationality?
    - Does your national legislation afford special social protection to maladjusted or socially disadvantaged children? (If so, please give details.)
    - Do children born out of wedlock have a special status under your country's legislation? (If so, please give details showing the differences that exist between the rights of children born in wedlock and those of children born out of wedlock.)
    - May a child belong to a sports, cultural or recreational association without the consent of his or her parents and, if so, from what age?
    - At what age may a child join a religious, political or trade-union organisation without the consent of his or her parents?
    - At what age may a child agree to a medical operation concerning him or her?
- Labour law
    - What special provisions concerning children are embodied in legislation on the right to work?

Childhood – a fundamental human right

We can all agree to define a child as a human being who has not yet reached the age of majority, while bearing in mind the differences in moral, intellectual and physical development of the various categories of children, adolescents and young people collectively referred to as children. The rights of the child should not, of course, be fundamentally different from those of the adult, but obviously the manner in which they are exercised may differ from one category of children to another.

A child needs a framework of values, normally transmitted by the family. In the course of his or her development he or she often goes through phases of opposition to parental authority, with potentially adverse consequences from which he or she must be protected. The laudable exercise of recognising that a child has rights as well as duties should not be allowed to obscure the fact that his or her "interests" must always take precedence. Similarly, a child has a right to childhood. Why expect him or her at any cost to be an adult before he or she is ready? The maturity of present-day children is in any case remarkable in comparison with that of previous generations of children. Their right to childhood should be preserved, just as the performance of parental duties and obligations should be accorded its proper place; parental authority should not be unduly undermined.

Only someone totally lacking in common sense would dispute the need for parents to exercise in everyday life certain decision-making powers on behalf of (even in opposition to) their children for their well-being (such as controlling their television viewing or having a say in their choice of friends). But thinking on the subject of parental duty should be pursued further. It is natural to feel some misgivings concerning the straightforward, unqualified grant of certain rights; for instance, in view of the vulnerability of young people to extremist political dogmas, it would be difficult to contemplate allowing children under the age of fifteen to join a political party. Similarly, the danger of sects and of the enrolment of idealistic and naive young people in questionable and unscrupulous groups supports the view that the choice of religion and religious observance should as a rule be left to the family, subject to the possibility for the child, from a certain age such as fifteen, of giving up his or her religion and opting for another.

Finally, enabling children, in the narrow and ordinary sense of the term, to avoid ending up on the official or unofficial labour market at a tender age is a way of recognising the fundamental right to a childhood.

Why we need an ombudsman for children – Sweden's experience

by Louise Sylwander,[1]

> "Children's ombudsman speaks out on child care spending cuts."
>
> "Children's ombudsman calls for ban on possession of kiddieporn videos."
>
> "Children's ombudsman slams jail for juveniles."

Brash headlines like these are the delight of Swedish media whenever I make a statement as Children's Ombudsman for Sweden. And I think this is also the way many people like to read about me. When the Office of the Children's Ombudsman was set up in Sweden, in 1993, there were great expectations of it really laying down the law – an independent, outspoken force capable of halting the deterioration in children's conditions which Sweden's economic problems had led to.

I have in fact tried to take upon myself this role of a persistent alarm bell, because I consider it one of my duties. But the official wording of my assignment gives me other roles to play as well. And personally I believe it takes more than alarmist manifestations

---

1. Louise Sylwander is Children's Ombudsman for Sweden. This contribution was drawn up at the request of the Social, Health and Family Affairs Committee of the Parliamentary Assembly of the Council of Europe.

if the children's ombudsman is to contribute towards genuine improvements.

I am the first holder of this position, to which I have been appointed for a 6-year period. My full official title is "Ombudsman for children and young persons", which is quite important really, because my assignment includes the whole population up to the age of 18. To help me I have a fourteen-strong secretariat.

The main task of the office which I represent is to assert the needs, rights and interests of children and young persons and to ensure that Sweden lives up to its commitments under the UN Convention on the Rights of the Child. That convention, then, is the document on which the activities of the children's ombudsman are based, and the convention too applies to everyone up to the age of 18.

Our task also includes disseminating the children's perspective of the convention at different levels of Swedish society. In practice, my work is very much concerned with taking part in public debate, forming opinion on major issues affecting children and young persons, and with conditioning the attitudes of society with regard to conditions for children and young persons.

A spokesman for children – the ongoing debate

The question of a special spokesman for children had been under discussion in the Swedish Riksdag ever since the 1980s. It formed the subject of several private members' bills, and the Norwegian children's ombudsman, established 12 years before, was frequently pointed to as an example.

The arguments in favour of setting up the Office of the Children's Ombudsman were that legal safeguards for children were felt to be neglected in Swedish society and that knowledge of children in medical services, social services and schools had been eviscerated. Several MPs referred to opinion formation and the need for active information activities on the subject of children's rights and interests. But it was Sweden's ratification of the United Nations Convention on the Rights of the Child, in 1990, which decided the Riksdag in favour of setting up the Office of the Children's Ombudsman and also determined the structure of the office itself.

The debate on the new office centred on two main questions: the wisdom of introducing yet another ombudsman in Sweden, since we have several already, and the statutory powers of the new ombudsman.

Unity on the need for a children's ombudsman

Sweden has an advanced system of ombudsmen, and the term itself has been applied to similar institutions set up in other countries. Sweden today has seven ombudsmen, responsible among other things for the supervision of public authorities, for consumer affairs, for equal opportunities and for the prevention of ethnic discrimination. During the debate on the Office of the Children's Ombudsman, fears were expressed of the ombudsman idea being watered down as a result of more and more groups in the community acquiring their own ombudsman for the protection of vested interests. This point of view was respected, but at the same time there was widespread agreement that children, on account of their exposure and vulnerability, ought to have an ombudsman of their own. Since my office was set up, an ombudsman for the disabled has been appointed and plans are well-advanced for appointing a special environmental ombudsman.

Working with the general or the particular?

As regards the powers of the children's ombudsman, the main question was whether the focus ought to be on generalities or particular cases. More exactly, the question was whether the office should be equipped with statutory powers of intervention in the

45

handling of individual cases. The alternative was to make the ombudsman an independent spokesman for children and young persons in a general sense, concentrating mainly on information and the moulding of public opinion. Some debaters felt that an ombudsman with no statutory powers of supporting individual children and youngsters would be powerless and be regarded as a cop-out for the government and Riksdag. And this way too, the ombudsman will have difficulty in addressing the intrinsically vital tasks of influencing public opinion. It was feared in particular that children and young persons would regard their own ombudsman as ineffective and would quickly lose interest in the whole idea.

But there were many arguments in favour of the order of things which materialised, namely that of a children's ombudsman charged with supervising the interests of children and young persons generally. The government found strong reasons of principle for segregating the respective assignments of the ombudsman, other national authorities and voluntary organisations. Sweden already had authorities whose task was to intervene for the protection and support of individual children and youngsters. Besides, the way in which these authorities discharge their duties comes under the scrutiny of a pre-existing ombudsman, the Parliamentary Ombudsman (JO for short). The government found it neither appropriate nor practical for similar duties to be vested in the children's ombudsman, because then there would be too great a risk of collisions and duplication.

A general assignment – guaranteeing the optimum use of resources

Another important viewpoint concerned getting the best out of the children's ombudsman's limited resources. Powers of intervention in particular cases could result in the secretariat being swamped with cases which were important but in which other authorities had already taken action and society had done what it could. Even in cases where individual children and youngsters had been badly treated by the authorities, supervisory bodies existed already. There are good reasons for supposing that the resources of the children's ombudsman are better occupied with trying to influence and modify the attitudes taken by authorities and other bodies to various questions by which children and young persons are affected.

Finally, the Riksdag decided that the children's ombudsman was to work in a very general field. This means that we have to consider children and young persons as a group and must induce the general public, authorities, companies and organisations to make provision for children's rights and interests in every conceivable connection. This does not mean that we ignore individual cases. On the contrary, actual cases of children in difficulty, or children subjected to conflicting decisions, can draw the attention of the children's ombudsman to unsatisfactory conditions and the absence of a children's perspective in a particular field. It is often with reference to particular questions that the children's ombudsman can highlight principles on which to base changes in the law or in official routines.

Three principal themes

Our work is guided by three principal themes:

– The United Nations Convention on the Rights of the Child;

– Children and young persons in difficulty;

– Young people's right of participation.

The United Nations Convention on the Rights of the Child is our guiding star – an important ideological instrument for asserting the children's perspective in different respects. The convention, though, is not directly applicable as Swedish law. Where international conventions are concerned, the system in Sweden is that new legislation has to be adapted to the commitments which various international agreements imply.

A Swedish rule which proves out of step with a convention has to be interpreted in what we call a treaty-friendly spirit. This means courts and authorities making active use, for example, of the Convention on the Rights of the Child and, as far as possible, interpreting Swedish laws and regulations in a way which is not at variance with the convention.

Before Sweden signed the convention, the government took stock of our legislation and came to the conclusion that there was good agreement between the articles of the convention and Swedish law. If anything, it was said, the shortcomings related to observance. Having worked a little more closely with these questions, though, I find deficiencies as regards the children's perspective and, above all, as regards children's opportunities of being given a hearing, both in the Social Services Act, in the Code of Parenthood and Guardianship and in the Aliens Act.

One of the ombudsman's important tasks, therefore, has been to systematically review legislation affecting children and propose amendments to bring Swedish law into line with Sweden's commitments under the convention. The children's perspective must be made a natural ingredient of all relevant new legislation. We go about this, for example, by taking part in consultation procedures on new legislation, making representations to government commissions and drafting legislation ourselves.

The main emphasis of this work is on the basic articles defining important principles. I refer above all to the ban on discrimination (Article 2), the principle of the child's best interests (Article 3), measures to give effect to the conventions (Article 4), the child's right to express an opinion and have it respected (Article 12) and the right to protection against abuse (Article 19).

It is encouraging to note that many of our viewpoints have recently been incorporated in draft new legislation, namely a new Social Services Bill and a new section in the Code of Parenthood and Guardianship. This is doubly gratifying, because it is the first time that basic principles from the United Nations Convention on the Rights of the Child have been directly incorporated in Swedish law. This success has inspired us to go further with the Aliens Act, as I began by describing, and with the rules of the Code of Parenthood and Guardianship concerning custody and access.

But the convention is not just for the guidance of legislators. The tasks of the Office of the Children's Ombudsman includes disseminating information and knowledge of the United Nations convention to the general public, professional categories working with children and decision-makers. I like to say that the convention is something which has to be lived. This means adults behaving towards children in such a way as to respect and sustain their full human dignity. It also means shaping society in such a way that children and young persons receive the protection and support they need in order for childhood and adolescence to have an intrinsic value.

The children's ombudsman is also very much involved in trying to implement the convention in local governments; in Sweden we have 286, because we think this is vital in order to promote children's rights and needs.

The second theme for the children's ombudsman is that of children in difficulty. In other words, we devote special attention to questions concerning children at risk. Even though children in Sweden are physically and mentally well off, especially compared with children in other countries, there are still many children in difficulty.

Although Swedish law in many fields is expressly concerned with children's best interests, much remains to be done in order to assert the children's perspective in practice. Victimisation and sexual abuse, for example, are matters of prime concern to the ombudsman.

The children's perspective is threatened, not least in periods of economic difficulty such as the one Sweden has been going through for some years now. As I see it, regardless of economic difficulties, Sweden must aim high. The United Nations Convention on the Rights of the Child requires states parties to make provision for children's needs, and I quote, "to the maximum extent of their available resources".

The third theme concerns the role of the children's ombudsman as spokesman for children and young persons. I think that my best way of representing young people is by trying to secure for them the opportunity of speaking for themselves and gaining respect for their opinions. This applies both in personal matters and in the community as a whole.

Within the Office of the Children's Ombudsman, therefore, we devote a good deal of time and labour to suggesting ways in which co-determination for children and young persons can be developed, for example in custody disputes and at local government level.

This business of letting children and young persons say their piece and giving them a hearing is the core of my perspective on children. Otherwise a children's ombudsman is very liable to lose sight of what children and young persons actually want. In the eager pursuit of change, one deceives oneself into thinking that one knows what is best for them. This, at best, is an adult perspective of children. In many cases it is also good for children and young persons, but this is not to be taken for granted; least of all by the children's ombudsman. A genuine child perspective focuses on the situation of the individual child. This is why our proposals are often based on giving children and young persons the opportunity of stating their views before decisions are made on matters affecting them.

As the children's representative, the children's ombudsman therefore has to gather knowledge and listen to young people in order to come up with the best possible suggestions. We keep in touch with children and young people in a variety of ways, for example by visiting schools, leisure centres or institutions.

For some time now we have also had a special telephone line which children and young persons up to the age of eighteen can use at very low cost. Known as "Children's Ombudsman Direct", it is primarily an information service. Children and young persons can phone up to speak their mind on different subjects and to bring things to the ombudsman's attention. They can be informed of their rights, of the United Nations convention and of the ombudsman's working methods. A special provision of the Secrecy Act enables the office to classify sensitive information, so that children and youngsters can turn to us in complete confidence.

In addition, we need to canvass the views and opinions of children and young persons more systematically on various matters, for example through research and attitude surveys. We are also investigating the potentialities of information technology for communicating with young persons.

Prioritisation is essential

With a field of operation as extensive as the children's ombudsman's, we have to prioritise and adopt a successive approach. Our priorities include – to mention only a few :

– information on the United Nations Convention on the Rights of the Child ;

- custody and access questions;
- victimisation in and out of school;
- the municipal children's perspective;
- participation of children and young persons;
- the situation of refugee children.

Co-operation with others is all part of the method

The Office of the Children's Ombudsman co-operates with a number and variety of authorities, organisations and individual persons. This improves our efficiency, gives us more punch, eliminates unnecessary duplication and – equally important – improves our knowledge and establishes a common perspective on different issues affecting children. Co-operation can assume a wide variety of forms. It can mean joint campaigns with voluntary organisations or co-operation with one or more authorities to develop a better children's perspective in the domain of the authority concerned. Or again it can mean setting up network or reference groups in a particular field. The office also has a co-ordinating role in relation to other authorities and institutions dealing with children's and young people's questions. Let me give you a few examples:

– the children's ombudsman has been made responsible for co-ordinating follow-up studies of different kinds concerning the social conditions of children and young persons. Various other authorities are involved in this work;

– together with other national authorities and organisations, the office also has the task of co-ordinating statistical data and compiling a statistical publication about children and young persons.

– the children's ombudsman also co-ordinates safety promotion activities for children and young persons. We have already run a fortnight's campaign, on the lines of Britain's Child Safety Week, aimed at highlighting the good work which is being done for the prevention of accidental injuries to children and young persons.

Government accountability –
a vital part of opinion formation

The children's ombudsman also has the task of reporting annually to the government. We use this report as an opinion-moulding instrument by trying in it to draw media attention to the questions which are raised. Among other things the report has to convey the ombudsman's views on how well Sweden has conformed during the year to the United Nations Convention on the Rights of the Child. The report also contains viewpoints and proposals which the ombudsman feels the government should consider.

All in all, the report can come to be a description of the status and development of the UN convention in Sweden from year to year. At the same time it provides the government with input documentation for its own reporting to the United Nations Committee on the Rights of the Child in Geneva, which has the task of monitoring different countries' compliance with the convention. Of course we also send our report to the committee in Geneva.

Points we have raised include the consequences for children and young persons of the heavy cuts in Swedish local government spending. Another principal issue concerns young people's right to influence, for example in schools and in local government. We proposed that it be made the duty of municipal authorities to find out children's and young people's opinions before deciding any question affecting them.

The government's report has attracted a great deal of interest and we hope that eventually it will become a central component of the Swedish debate on conditions for children. But we cannot rely on the government's report alone. As I hinted earlier, we employ a whole variety of instruments. The children's ombudsman is of course consulted on any number of proposals which may result in changes in the law.

Experience has shown, though, that you have to get in on the ground floor, as it were. Once a government commission's proposals are cut and dried, there is not usually much scope left for allowing for the needs of children. So we also employ more informal methods, such as lobbying a commission before its proposals are presented. I have already mentioned work on the Aliens Act as an example of this kind.

Another way of drawing attention to a question is by arranging hearings with experts capable of illuminating the child's perspective. Letters to other authorities and also to the government has sometimes produced rapid results. The important thing is to find the appropriate measure for each particular situation and to keep up the pressure even if no immediate response is forthcoming. Disseminating the child's perspective is very much a matter of conditioning and changing attitudes, which calls for long-termism and perseverance. But, I think it's worth the effort. And I cannot think of a finer job than being in the front line for children and young persons.

Putting a face to children's rights

Even in Sweden, children and young persons have neither self-determination nor voting rights, and they have few other channels for conveying their opinions to the people who make the decisions. Children and young persons have difficulty in making their voices heard and in articulating their needs.

Children's interests in the life of the community often have to defer to the interests of adults. Even if children express their opinions, they are seldom treated with the same respect as those of adults.

They have very little opportunity for taking part in public debate or of influencing their situation to the extent which their interests and knowledge justify. Political debaters, consequently, most often speak about children and young persons, at best they may speak to them, but it is very seldom indeed that they speak with them.

The children's perspective, then, needs to be promoted on a more systematic and efficient basis. In order for children's and young people's rights, needs and interests to attract sufficient attention, somebody must speak up for them and defend their cause: a special advocate, giving the rights of children and young persons a "face" and capable of viewing social developments in their perspective.

Surveillance of this kind is also fully in line with the commitment entailed by the United Nations Convention on the Rights of the Child. That convention and the world summit that followed it were greeted with such euphoria that it is all too easy to assume that the convention itself represents the final word on children's rights. This leads to the question of enforcement. The convention makes provision for the establishment of a committee on the rights of the child. The principal function of the new committee is to operate the system of periodic reporting provided for by the convention.

The committee may make "suggestions and general recommendations" based on information received. There is not provision for interstate complaints or individual complaints. The only implementation mechanism is therefore the reporting procedure. Whether this is successful depends on the quality of reports submitted by states, the range and quality of outside information submitted and the ability of the committee.

But to get all the relevant information, to help prevent bias or neglect of significant problem areas, many countries will find it necessary to establish child-oriented institutions on a national level.

They will act as mechanisms whose specific task is to act as watch-dogs for children's rights and monitor the situation of children against the international criteria now laid down – institutions which will probe and question both existing and mooted laws and prac-tices, which will examine critically the impact of structures and designs of everyday lives of children, such as schools, courts, neglect and abuse proceedings.

In most countries, though, responsibility for conditions with an impact on children is divided between ministries and local adminis-trative offices. With little contact between them, practically water-tight barriers may exist between different sectors responsible for various aspects of children's lives and welfare.

We now have an important international instrument to secure bet-ter respect for children's rights. Experience from other fields has shown that rights cannot simply be declared or agreed upon – they must also be monitored and safeguarded. I think that the real value of the convention can only be demonstrated by our own ability to ensure its effective implementation. In this context, a national commissioner or an ombudsman for children and youth could prove vital for the promotion of children's rights.

Applying the main international treaties

The European Convention on Human Rights

By ratifying the European Convention on Human Rights governments reaffirm their profound belief in those fundamental freedoms, civil and political rights which are the foundation of justice and peace in the world, and which are best maintained by an effective political democracy and by a common understanding and observance of human rights. In view of its evolving and rich case-law, the Convention became "law-making", and a "living instrument" with a clear impact on the legal systems of all Council of Europe member states, and a reaffirmed value for all those who are victims of the violation of their fundamental human rights and freedoms, including children.

Nearly all member states have also ratified the International Covenant on Civil and Political Rights of the United Nations, which states:

"1. Every child shall have, without any discrimination as to race, colour, sex, language, religion, national or social origin, property of birth, the right to such measures of protection as are required by his status as a minor, on the part of his family, society and the state.

2. Every child shall be registered immediately after birth and shall have a name.

3. Every child has the right to acquire a nationality."

This provision or a similar one might be included in the European Convention on Human Rights. Such inclusion would have the obvious advantage of effective implementation of this right through the European Commission and Court of Human Rights in Strasbourg.

The European Convention on Human Rights applies to all individuals who happen to be on the territory or are otherwise under the jurisdiction of one of the contracting states. This universal character of the Convention has been confirmed by the European Commission and Court of Human Rights in a certain number of cases concerning military staff, psychiatric patients and others. The Convention does not exclude these categories of population or any other, nor does it provide a particular protection to a certain group which it does not grant to another.

On the other hand, Article 14 of the Convention provides that the enjoyment of the rights and freedoms of the Convention must "be secured without discrimination on any ground such as sex, race, colour, language, religion, political or other opinion, national or social origin, association with a national minority, property, birth or other status".[1] This enumeration does not include a discrimination or a distinction[2] based on age.

From the above one may draw two conclusions with regard to children. Firstly, the Convention applies to children; and secondly, although children are entitled to enjoy the human rights listed in the Convention, the restrictions which member states may impose on the exercise of these rights by children do no necessarily have to be

---

1. In accordance with the wording of Article 14 this provision is not an autonomous one; in other words it can only be applied in relation to an article listed in the Convention. Order No. 443 (1988) instructs the "Legal Affairs Committee, with the aid of the Committee on Migration, Refugees and Demography, to investigate possibilities of extending Article 14 of the European Convention on Human Rights, and to submit detailed proposals in this connection as appropriate".
2. *Distinction* is the word used in the French text of Article 14.

the same as those imposed on adults – provided, of course, that these restrictions are always in conformity with the Convention which itself indicates the limits. For instance, "freedom to manifest one's religion or beliefs shall be subject only to such limitations as are prescribed by law and are necessary in a democratic society in the interests of public safety, for the protection of public order, health or morals, or for the protection of the rights and freedoms of others".[1]

The jurisprudence of the European Commission and Court of Human Rights confirms that children have to face practical and psychological hurdles before they can bring cases before the Commission. There is a general lack of knowledge about the Convention even among lawyers. The situation of children being taken into public care has repeatedly been dealt with by the organs of the Convention. Their case-law indicates that children need to be involved in the decision-making process as regards their situation.[2]

Returning to the wording of Article 24 of the United Nations covenant one notes that, in its first paragraph, it introduces a right which is not included in the European Convention on Human Rights, that is, the right to measures of protection, a right which is granted to children only. There is, of course, nothing against such a basic right to protection but one may wonder whether it should not be extended to the aged, the sick, the poor, the disabled, psychiatric patients and all other people in our society who may be in need of special protection.

It may seem relevant in this context to mention that there are provisions for the protection of workers, mothers, children, young people, and so on in the European Social Charter. Some of the

---

1. Article 9, paragraph 2.
2. See the contribution by Mr Buquicchio-de-Boer on "Children and the European Convention on Human Rights: a survey of case-law of the European Commission and Court of Human Rights" in Studies in Honour of Gerard J. Wiarda, 1988, and his statement at the hearing.

provisions of the charter may usefully be included in the European Convention on Human Rights and thus be brought under the supervision of the European Commission and Court of Human Rights as our Assembly proposed in its Recommendation 838 (1978). In that recommendation the Assembly considered that in order to be incorporated in the Convention any right must be fundamental and enjoy general recognition and be capable of sufficiently precise definition to lay legal obligations on a state, rather than simply constitute a general rule.

In a 1987 report by the Centre for Socio-legal Studies, the authors noted the following:

"The Convention is, as we put it 'adult-oriented'. Although children can take the benefit of the general provisions of the Convention applicable to all persons, their specific requirements as children are nowhere explicitly recognised. Hence, when procedures for intervention are discussed (Article 6), it is almost always from the point of view of the protection given to the parents, not the children. When 'respect for family life' is at issue under Article 8, it is almost always the family life of the parents, rather than that of the children which is given dominance. Although states are permitted, under the Convention, to intervene in family life (as understood, that of the parent) to protect children (and even this is not as explicit under Article 8 as it might be) there is no requirement that they should do so, and hence no real protection under the Convention for children subjected to the powers of parents which are recognised under private law. We therefore urge that attention continue to be given to finding ways in which the Convention might be extended into the area of children's rights."[1]

1. Report prepared by MM. John Eekelaar and Robert Dingwall of the Centre for Socio-Legal Studies, Wolfson College, Oxford, United Kingdom, at the request of the Secretary General on the replies of governments to the enquiry under Article 57 of the European Convention on Human Rights concerning the

Introducing special provisions for the protection of children, for instance by adopting an additional protocol to the Convention, would make the system of protection too legal. Ways should, however, be found to facilitate access of children to information on their rights and how they may exercise their rights. The European Commission of Human Rights accepted the right of children to introduce complaints without the authority of their legal representative and such a right is, of course, essential when the issue at stake concerns a conflict with that representative.[2] Generally speaking, the Convention is not ineffective as regards the protection of children.

The second paragraph of Article 24 of the international covenant, which provides that every child shall be registered immediately after birth and shall have a name, is unlikely to raise problems or objections in any Council of Europe member states. It confirms the situation which already exists.

The third paragraph of Article 24 of the covenant provides that every child has the right to acquire a nationality. Nationality is an invention of mankind. Yet its importance is so great that it is not an exaggeration to include the right to a nationality in a catalogue of fundamental human rights. In fact a person without a nationality is seriously handicapped in our modern societies, and whatever possible must be done to avoid cases of statelessness. While fully subscribing to the principle that everybody should be able to have a nationality, here are a few observations on the United Nations text:

– it singles out children, whereas the right to a nationality is equally fundamental to adults;

---

implementation of the European Convention on Human Rights in respect of children and young people placed in care or in institutions following a decision of the administrative or judicial authorities (Doc. H/SG (87) 1, paragraph 17).
2. Application No. 6753/74, 19 December 1974.

– under the system of the European Convention on Human Rights the fundamental rights listed can be invoked against a contracting state. The right to acquire a nationality might be exercised against the state on the territory of which a stateless child may happen to be. The concept of territory includes ships and aeroplanes. Does this mean that, as soon as a stateless child travels in a plane, it has the right to acquire the nationality of the state where the plane is registered?

– the United Nations Covenant does not state the conditions under which a child may be able to acquire a nationality (for instance: birth on the national territory of the contracting state, prolonged residence, impossibility to obtain any other nationality, a special fee, language or school requirements, etc.);

– the provision, if listed in the European Convention on Human Rights might be worded as follows: "Any person, born on the territory of a contracting state who has not acquired a nationality through his parents or otherwise, has the right to acquire the nationality of that state". Although seemingly attractive, this solution may also have the disadvantage of disrupting the unity of the family. For instance, a child born from stateless parents would get the nationality of the state where it is born but its parents and brothers and sisters would remain stateless. Problems may arise here, especially when the family decides to move to another country.

The European Social Charter

The European Social Charter is the pendant of the European Convention on Human Rights with regard to the protection of economic and social rights. It is one of the main Council of Europe instruments in respect of children. The right of children and young people to protection is elaborated in detail in Article 7 of the charter. Other provisions of importance to children in the European

Social Charter are Article 9 on the right to vocational guidance, Article 10, paragraph 2, on a system of apprenticeship for training young boys and girls; Article 16, on the right of the family to social, legal and economic protection; Article 17, on the right of mothers and children to social and economic protection; and Article 19, paragraph 6, on the reunification of the family of a migrant worker. These provisions assure the protection of children and adolescents in the workplace as well as the protection of those without any link to the working environment.

The draft revised Social Charter, drawn up by the Committee on the European Social Charter which, between 1990 and 1994 was entrusted with the relaunching of the charter, is due to be adopted soon by the Committee of Ministers and opened for signature by Council of Europe member states.[1] The draft revised charter increases the protection of young people at work and reinforces their protection outside the workplace. In addition, taking into account the importance of the right of children and adolescents to protection, the revised charter adds Article 7 to the main body of the charter.[2]

The protection of young people at work consists in prohibiting their employment under a certain age while authorising certain types of work, and in determining their working conditions as well as a number of other guarantees.

The charter sets at 15 the minimum age for admission to employment (Article 7, paragraph 1) and sets a higher minimum age for

---

1. Situation as of 1 March 1996.

2. It is possible to enter only partially into the committments contained in Part II of the charter. However, certain provisions (referred to as the "compulsory nucleus") which are considered to be particularly important must be accepted upon ratification of the charter: Article 20, paragraph 1, of the charter and Article A, paragraph 1, of the draft revised charter.

admission to certain determined occupations considered as dangerous or unhealthy (Article 7, paragraph 2), the case law of the Committee of Independent Experts of the European Social Charter sets the age at 18 for certain activities (for example work which involves contact with benzene). The draft revised charter generalises this solution. As to authorised work before the minimum age for admission to employment, it can only be prescribed light work with no risk of adverse effects on children's health, morals or education (Article 7, paragraph 1) and, for children still subject to compulsory schooling, work which enables them to derive the full benefit from this education (Article 7, paragraph 3).

The working conditions laid down by the Charter concern the limitation of working hours of workers aged under 16 (Article 7, paragraph 4 – in the draft revised charter this provision is intended for workers under 18 years of age), remuneration of young workers and apprentices (Article 7, paragraph 5), the inclusion in the working day of the time spent in vocational training during the normal working hours with the consent of the employer (Article 7, paragraph 6), annual holiday with pay (Article 7, paragraph 7 – the draft revised charter increases the current allowance of three weeks to four) and prohibition of night work for workers under 18 years of age (Article 7, paragraph 8).

This protection of young persons at work is completed by two other guarantees; the regular medical control of workers under 19 years of age employed in certain occupations prescribed by national laws or regulations (Article 7, paragraph 9) and special protection against the physical and moral dangers to which children and adolescents are exposed, and particularly against those resulting directly or indirectly from their work (Article 7, paragraph 10).

To this protection of young persons at work is added protection for those without any connection to the working environment:

protection against physical and moral dangers, the protection of young offenders and special protection with regard to health. The draft revised charter reinforces certain of these guarantees and adds others.

The protection of young persons against physical and moral dangers outside the working environment is ensured by the adverb "particularly" used in Article 7, paragraph 10. The dangers which young people face have evolved. The perceived dangers have traditionally been alcoholism, drug abuse, pornography, and the recent danger posed by Aids. Now physical abuse must be added, including that of a sexual nature.

Very concerned about the protection needed by young persons, and conscious that this protection can be necessary even within the family, the committee of independent experts decided to expand its control over three aspects of the protection of young persons that it considers at present to have priority: the ill-treatment inflicted on young people, both within and outside the family with emphasis on the real importance of this problem and measures taken or envisaged to remedy the situation; the access of these young people to civil and criminal courts, *inter alia* when there are family conflicts, and also the situation of young delinquents which requires particular attention.

As regards the protection of juvenile delinquents in the charter, this is mostly concerned with special institutions and courts. At present the charter also deals with the age at which criminal responsibility is set and the age at which sanctions may be pronounced, what sanctions may be applied and their forms of enforcement, as well as measures of protection, education and health care provided and effectively implemented.

With regard to health, Article 11 of the charter on the right to protection of health, deals with, *inter alia*, perinatal and infant healthcare. In addition, Article 8, paragraph 3, which guarantees work breaks – included in working time and paid as such – for mothers to nurse their infants, in practice allows mothers to continue nursing beyond the time allocated for maternity leave.

The draft revised charter establishes, in a new Article 17, the right of children and adolescents to social, legal and economic protection. This provision carries a package of measures, whose goal is to enable the young to grow up in an environment conducive to the full development of their personality and of their physical and mental capacities. Besides the care, the assistance, the education and the training young people need, these measures expressly guarantee the protection of the young against negligence, violence or exploitation, special protection for young people deprived of their family's support, together with free primary and secondary education and regular school attendance.

These provisions apply to young people as such,[1] though they do, in part, concern the protection of young people within the family. Young people are also protected as members of a family, on the one hand by the provisions concerning the status of the child and, on the other, by the protective measures specific to family life.[2]

The United Nations Convention on the Rights of the Child

The impact of the United Nations Convention on the Rights of the Child in this important area is undeniable. The adoption of this instrument was a clear landmark in the field of human rights, for the political consensus it has built around children, for the new vision it

---

1. See *Children and adolescents*, "Social Charter Monographs", No. 3 (To be published in 1996).

2. See *The Family*, "Social Charter Monographs", No. 1.

brings of childhood, and for the new place it gives to children in today's society. Such a reality is undoubtedly confirmed by the unprecedented number of states, from Europe and elsewhere, who have become parties to it. Ratification of this convention is universal, with the exception of five countries (namely the United Arab Emirates, the United States, Oman, Somalia and Switzerland).

Summary of the main provisions[1]

Preamble

The preamble recalls the basic principles of the United Nations and specific provisions of certain relevant human rights treaties and proclamations; it reaffirms the fact that children, because of their vulnerability, need special care and protection; and it places special emphasis on the primary caring and protective repsponsibility of the family, the need for legal and other protection of the child before and after birth, the importance of respect for the cultural values of the child's community, and the vital role of international co-operation in achieving the realisation of children's rights.

Definition of a child

All people under the age of 18, unless by law majority is attained at an earlier age.

Non-discrimination

Non-discrimination is the principle that all rights apply to all children without exception, and the state's obligation to protect children from any form of discrimination. The state must take positive action to promote all children's rights and must not violate any of them.

---

1. Reproduced from the third edition of the "Briefing Kit" produced by Defence for Children International (DCI) and the United Nations Children's Fund (Unicef) (May 1989).

The best interests of the child

All actions concerning the child should take full account of his or her best interests. The state must provide adequate care when parents or others responsible fail to do so.

Implementation of rights

The state's obligation to translate the rights in the convention into reality.

Parental guidance and the child's evolving capacities

The state's duty to respect the rights and responsibilities of parents and the wider family to provide guidance appropriate to the child's evolving capacities.

Survival and development

The child's inherent right to life, and the state's obligation to ensure his or her survival and development.

Name and nationality

The right to have a name from birth and to be granted a nationality.

Preservation of identity

The state's obligation to protect and, if necessary, re-establish the basic aspects of a child's identity (name, nationality and family ties).

Separation from parents

The child's right to live with his or her parents unless this is deemed incompatible with his or her best interests; the right to maintain contact with both parents if separated from one or both; the state's duties in cases where such separation results from state action.

Family reunification

The right of children and their parents to leave any country and to enter their own in order to be reunited or to maintain the child-parent relationship.

Illicit transfer and non-return

The state's obligation to try to prevent and /or remedy the kidnapping or retention of children abroad by a parent or third party.

The child's opinion

The child's right to express an opinion, and to have that opinion taken into account, in any matter or procedure affecting the child.

Freedom of expression

The child's right to obtain and make known information, and to express his or her views, unless this would violate the rights of others.

Freedom of thought, conscience and religion

The child's right to freedom of thought, conscience and religion, subject to appropriate parental guidance and national law.

Freedom of association

The right of children to meet with others and to join or set up associations unless the fact of doing so violates the rights of others.

Protection of privacy

The right to protection from interference with privacy, family and correspondence, and from libel or slander.

Access to appropriate information

The role of the media in disseminating information to children that is consistent with the moral well-being and knowledge and understanding among peoples, and which respects the child's cultural background. The state is to take measures to encourage this and to protect children from harmful materials.

Parental responsibilities

The principle that both parents have joint primary responsibility for bringing up their children, and that the state should support them in this task.

Protection from abuse and neglect

The state's obligation to protect children from all forms of maltreatment perpretrated by parents or others responsible for their care, and to undertake preventive and treatment programmes in this regard.

Protection of children without families

The state's obligation to provide special protection for children deprived of their family environment and to ensure that appropriate alternative family care or institutional placement is made available to them, taking into account the child's cultural background.

Adoption

In countries where adoption is recognised and/or allowed, it shall only be carried out in the best interests of the child, with all necessary safeguards for a given child and authorisation by the competent authorities.

Refugee children

Special protection to be granted to children who are refugees or seeking refugee status, and the state's obligation to co-operate with competent organisations providing such protection and assistance.

Handicapped children

The right of handicapped children to special care, education and training designed to help them to achieve the greatest possible self-reliance and to lead a full and active life in society.

Health and health services

The right to the highest level of health possible and to access to health and medical services, with special emphasis on primary and preventive health care, public health education and the diminution of infant mortality. The state's obligation to work towards the abolition of harmful traditional practices. Emphasis is laid on the need for international co-operation to ensure this right.

Periodic review of placement

The right of children placed by the state for reasons of care, protection or treatment to have all aspects of that placement evaluated regularly.

Social security

The right of children to benefit from social security.

Standard of living

The right of children to benefit from an adequate standard of living, the primary responsibility of parents to provide this, and the state's duty to ensure that this responsibility is first fulfillable and then fulfilled, where necessary through the recovery of maintenance.

Education

The child's right to education, and the state's duty to ensure that primary education at least is made free and compulsory. Administration of school discipline is to reflect the child's human dignity. Emphasis is laid on the need for international co-operation to ensure this right.

Aims of education

The state's recognition that education should be directed at developing the child's personality and talents, preparing the child for active life as an adult, fostering respect for basic human rights and developing respect for the child's own cultural and national values and those of others.

Children of minorities or indigenous populations

The right of children of minority communities and indigenous populations to enjoy their own culture and to practise their own religion and language.

Leisure, recreation and cultural activities

The right of children to leisure, play and participation in cultural and artistic activities.

Child labour

The state's obligation to protect children from engaging in work that constitutes a threat to their health, education or development, to set minimum ages for employment, and to regulate conditions of employment.

Drug abuse

The child's right to protection from the use of narcotic and psychotropic drugs and from being involved in their production or distribution.

Sexual exploitation

The child's right to protection from sexual exploitation and abuse, including prostitution and involvement in pornography.

Sale, trafficking and abduction

The state's obligation to make every effort to prevent the sale, trafficking and abduction of children.

Other forms of exploitation

The child's right to protection from all other forms of exploitation not covered in Articles 32, 33, 34 and 35.

Torture and deprivation of liberty

The prohibition of torture, cruel treatment or punishment, capital punishment, life imprisonment, and unlawful arrest or deprivation of liberty. The principles of appropriate treatment, separation from detained adults, contact with the family and access to legal and other assistance.

Armed conflicts

The obligation of states to respect and ensure respect for humanitarian law as it applies to children. The principle that no child under the age of 15 take a direct part in hostilities or be recruited into the armed forces, and that all children affected by armed conflict benefit from protection and care.

Rehabilitative care

The state's obligation to ensure that child victims of armed conflicts, torture, neglect, maltreatment or exploitation receive appropriate treatment for their recovery and social reintegration.

Administration of juvenile justice

The right of children alleged or recognised as having committed an offence to respect for their human rights and, in particular, to benefit from all aspects of the due process of law, including legal or other assistance in preparing and presenting their defence. The principle that recourse to judicial proceedings and institutional placements should be avoided wherever possible and appropriate.

Respect for existing standards

The principle that, if any standards set in national law or other applicable international instruments are higher than those of this convention, it is the higher standard that applies.

Implementation and entry into force

The provisions of Articles 42-54 notably foresee:

i.   the state's obligation to make the rights contained in this convention widely known to both adults and children;

ii. the setting up of a committee on the rights of the child composed of ten experts, which will consider reports that states parties to the convention are to submit two years after ratification and every five years thereafter. The convention enters into force – and the committee would therefore be set up – when twenty countries have ratified it;

iii. states parties are to make their reports widely available to the general public;

iv. the committee may propose that special studies be undertaken on specific issues relating to the rights of the child, and may make its evaluations known to each state party concerned as well as to the United Nations General Assembly;

v. in order to "foster the effective implementation of the convention and to encourage international co-operation", the specialised agencies of the United Nations (such as the ILO, WHO and Unesco) and Unicef would be able to attend the meetings of the committee. Together with any other body recognised as "competent", including NGOs in consultative status with the United Nations and United Nations organs such as the UNHCR, they can submit pertinent information to the committee and be asked to advise on the optimal implementation of the convention.

Other important conventions

Application of the European Convention on Recognition and Enforcement of Decisions concerning Custody of Children and on Restoration of Custody of Children (1980) should provide a rapid means of settling the growing number of disputes over children between divorced or separated parents. These often lead to the abduction of a child to another country or breaches of access orders involving refusal to return a child to the parent who has been granted custody. The convention is based on four principles:

- free, rapid, non-bureaucratic assistance from the authorities to trace and return a child who has been improperly removed;
- consideration of the well-being of the child concerned;
- mutual recognition of foreign child custody orders;
- judicial safeguards for the legitimate interest of both parents as regards custody of their children and access to them.

Under the convention a child will be returned through the intermediary of a special body set up for the purpose in each state – if the child has been improperly removed and if a request for return is made within six months of the removal.

The conventions of the International Labour Organisation (ILO) are also of importance in respect of children. They concern working conditions, the abolition of forced labour, equality of work, non-discrimination between workers, trade-union freedom and freedom of collective bargaining, the fight against child labour, the minimum age for admission to employment, etc. At the end of 1988 the International Labour Office had adopted no less than 168 conventions, many of which require more ratifications by Council of Europe member states. Particular attention may be given to Convention No. 138 of 1973 of the minimum age for admission to employment.

The European Convention on the Exercise of Children's Rights

The European Convention on the Exercise of Children's Rights was opened for signature by member states on 25 January 1996.[1] The draft convention had been submitted to the Parliamentary Assembly for an opinion. It is based on the understanding that children should be respected as individuals and should be assigned a greater measure of autonomy in judicial proceedings affecting them. The convention grants children a certain minimum of procedural rights in some family proceedings and creates mechanisms for the promotion and exercise of these rights.

The Assembly welcomed the draft convention, and was convinced that it would contribute to strengthening the position of children in court. However, it was the view of the Assembly that some amendments to the draft text were necessary in order to make the convention more powerful.

The convention tries not to duplicate other universal or regional texts on children's rights. Since a number of important international instruments have dealt extensively with children's substantive rights – the United Nations International Convention on the Rights of the Child being of primary importance in this regard – the convention focuses on children's procedural rights and on the exercise of these rights. In this, the instrument attempts to fill in the

---

1. The text of this convention can be found in the appendix.

implementation gap in the international legal framework of children's rights.

General characteristics of the European Convention on the Exercise of Children's Rights

Scope and object of the convention

The convention does not deal with substantive children's rights. Since most of the Council of Europe member states are signatories to the United Nations International Convention on the Rights of the Child, the aim had been to avoid restating the principles laid down in the United Nations document. Instead, the convention endeavours to support and supplement the United Nations convention and to contribute to its effective implementation.

The object of the convention, as stated in Article 1, paragraph 2, is "in the best interests of children, to promote their rights, grant them procedural rights and to facilitate the exercise of these rights by ensuring that children are, themselves, or through other persons or bodies, informed and allowed to participate in the proceedings before a judicial authority affecting them". Proceedings before a judicial authority affecting children are defined as family proceedings such as those involving the exercise of parental responsibilities, in particular residence of and access to children (Article 1, paragraph 3).

The convention is very flexible with regard to the conditions for ratification. Each state shall specify at least three family proceedings to which the convention shall apply at the time of signature or ratification. The explanatory report to the convention provides a non-exhaustive list of proceedings which may be specified by states to be family proceedings. It includes proceedings like: custody; residence; access to children; questions of parentage; legitimacy; adoption; legal guardianship; administration of property of children; care procedure, and removal of parental responsibilities.

Although the list of examples is said to be non-exhaustive the scope of the convention remains limited by the term "family proceedings".

The procedural rights granted by the convention can be exercised in proceedings before a judicial authority affecting children. In Article 2, however, the concept of "proceedings before a judicial authority affecting children" is narrowly defined. Only family proceedings such as those involving the exercise of parental responsibilities, residence and access to children in particular, are covered by the scope of the convention (Article 1, paragraph 3).

The convention further leaves it to the member states to specify those types of family proceedings affecting children (at least three) to which the convention shall apply.

The convention keeps silent with regard to the possible procedural rights of children to exercise other fundamental substantive rights recognised by the United Nations convention, like the right to freedom of expression, the right to freedom of religion, etc.

It would appear that the authors of the draft have been guided by the desire to attract the highest possible number of ratifications, believing that it is better to have a viable legal instrument limited in scope, than an ambitious document, remaining a dead letter. The convention also provides for a number of opportunities for "autonomous" post-ratification developments. The parties are free to confer additional procedural rights to children and to broaden the scope of application of the convention. A flexible procedure for amendment of the convention is envisaged through the mediation of the Standing Committee. Thus, the convention relies on a gradual approach.

Although there is much common sense in this approach, it is still regrettable that the convention should opt for the principle of the "lowest common denominator". In the opinion of the Committee on Legal Affairs and Human Rights it is essential that all contracting states accept a certain minimum of procedural rights applicable to important proceedings affecting children.

Procedural rights

The following main procedural rights are granted to children by the convention: the right to be informed and to express their views in proceedings (Article 3), and the right to apply for the appointment of a special representative where the holders of parental responsibilities are precluded from representing the child as a result of a conflict of interest (Article 4).

States are also urged to consider granting additional procedural rights to children, for example the right to be assisted by an appropriate person of their choice in order to help them express their views; the right to apply, themselves or through other persons or bodies, for the appointment of a separate representative, in appropriate cases a lawyer; the right to appoint their own representative; the right to exercise some or all of the rights of parties to such proceedings (Article 5).

It might be necessary to note that the legislations of most member states already grant such rights to children in some family proceedings. In the process of drafting its Recommendation 1121 (1990), the Parliamentary Assembly conducted a study on the legislation affecting children in force in different member states. It appeared that in many member states procedural rules exist guaranteeing that children's voices are heard in family proceedings. For instance the law of most member states grants to children of a certain age the possibility of giving their opinion in the divorce proceedings of their parents.[1] The same is valid for the role of the child when being

---

1. This applies for children over 10 years in Austria and over 12 years in Belgium, Denmark, Netherlands, Norway and Spain. Children should be asked for their opinion if it is evident that they cannot be harmed by being questioned.

placed in an institution or a foster family. In most countries children over 12 have the right to be heard in such proceedings. It is, therefore, doubtful whether the draft convention will introduce substantial improvement in the existing national rules for the exercise of children's rights in family proceedings.

At the same time, the convention does not discuss the very controversial but important issue of granting children the possibility of initiating legal proceedings themselves and of asserting certain rights independently of or even against the will of their parents. Admittedly, this is an extremely sensitive area, where the exercise of rights should be combined with satisfactory guarantees that the best interests of children are protected. Yet the complexity of the problem should not mean avoiding it.

The role of judicial authorities

An important merit of the convention is that it endeavours to guarantee the practical realisation of children's procedural rights through creating corresponding obligations and powers for the judiciary. Several duties are placed on the judicial authorities: to ensure that children have sufficient information and to consult children unless this is manifestly contrary to their best interests (Article 6) as well as to act speedily in proceedings affecting the child (Article 7). The convention further authorises the judicial authority to act on its own motion where the welfare of a child is seriously in danger, this prerogative being, however, limited only to cases determined by internal law.

Implementation

To assure the effective implementation of the convention, the text proposes that a standing committee be set up. The committee shall consist of one or more representatives of each party to the convention, each party having one vote. It shall be empowered to keep the problems relating to the convention under review and to adopt recommendations.

"Having sufficient understanding"

The procedural rights are assigned in many cases only to children "considered by internal law as having sufficient understanding". By leaving it to internal law to define when children have sufficient understanding, the convention opens a broad space for conflicting interpretations which may impede the effective implementation of the convention. Indeed, most member states' legislations do not contain precise definitions of this concept. It is often a task for the judiciary to decide on a case-by-case basis. Nevertheless, some guidelines for the interpretation of this concept should have been given by the convention in order to assure its uniform implementation.

National bodies

The convention takes up an idea furthered by the Parliamentary Assembly in its Recommendation 1121 (1990) which envisaged the appointment of a special ombudsman for children, who could inform them on their rights, counsel them, intervene and, possibly, take legal action on their behalf (see section 12.e.ii of the recommendation).

The convention does not use the term "ombudsman", but speaks more generally of "national bodies for promotion and exercise of children's rights". The parties are free to choose the appropriate type of structure, whether there should be one or more such bodies, whether they should be private or public, and so on.

The convention applies some caution when specifying the functions of these bodies. The emphasis is on giving proposals and opinions on child-related legislation, providing information and seeking the views of children. It is disappointing that key functions like intervening and taking legal action on behalf of children are not envisaged.

Monitoring

The convention assigns significant authority to the Standing Committee (Chapter III of the convention). This committee shall consider questions of interpretation and implementation of the convention and may issue recommendations and propose amendments to the convention. It may be desirable to set forth explicitly an additional function of the committee, namely to request parties to produce national reports on the compliance of their legislation with the provisions of the convention.

Given the important role of the committee, higher requirements may be stipulated for the selection procedure of committee members. It is the view of the Assembly that the committee would be better equipped to perform its tasks if it consisted of independent experts. The procedure for election might be similar to the one for the United Nations Committee on the Rights of the Child.[1]

Background

The convention cannot be regarded as an isolated instrument, but should be placed in the context of the ongoing debate on children's rights and evaluated in the light of past accomplishments in this field.

Concepts of children's rights

At first glance there is nothing to argue about on children's rights. Everyone would agree that children should enjoy a happy childhood, that they should be spared the hardships of poverty,

---

1. See Article 43, United Nations International Convention on the Rights of the Child.

social disaster and war. We would all wish that children were surrounded by care and affection.

However, under this surface of seeming unanimity a large spectrum of views on children's rights can be identified. Indeed, the international community has recognised that children do have rights. The problems start when it comes to defining the scope and the meaning of these rights. The differences are not only technical but are based on different philosophies on the rights of children. The conflicting views may be summarised under two main concepts on children's rights, that is the welfare appraoch and the autonomy approach. The welfare model points out children's limited capacity for acting rationally and emphasises the need for intensified protection, both on behalf of parents and of society. In contrast, the autonomy approach argues that most children are as capable to make rational choices as adults and should be allowed to take part in the decision-making processes affecting them.

In fact, very few people would subscribe to an extreme version of either approach. The development of the children's rights discussion may therefore be described as a search for reconciliation and balance between protection and autonomy.

The protective approach to children was the first to evolve and has always been less disputable. It is at the core of basic children-related legislation at both national and international level. It was at the second stage and with more caution that national and international decision-makers acknowledged the need for more autonomy for children. Since laws are tabled by adults, it had been difficult for them to voluntarily surrender part of their dominant position in the children-parents relationship.

Seen in this context, the draft convention attempts to assign a greater measure of autonomy to children in family proceedings affecting them, while taking into account the possible risks for children's welfare.

A pan-European strategy for children

As citizens in present-day society and representatives of tomorrow's society, children have rights, which are essential to their protection and to securing the best opportunities for developing the full range of their potential.

These rights are indivisible and universal, that is of equal value and validity throughout the world. They must apply to all children without discrimination on any ground, regardless of nationality, sex, race, disability, religion, legal status or culture.

Children are fully-fledged citizens with rights and responsibilities (to themselves, family and society). Their views must be heard and considered in decision-making which affects them. They should be able to take on greater responsibility, autonomy and self-determination as they mature and their capacities evolve.

The best interests of the child must be a guiding principle of all action that affects children either directly or indirectly (for example, fiscal or environmental measures).

Increasing global interdependence is a feature of the modern world, and practical and ethical considerations demand that children's rights be made a reality outside Europe, too. Promoting the universal implementation of the United Nations convention, appropriate policies and increased development assistance should provide the main practical expression of Europe's solidarity and responsibility towards children in developing countries.

Making children's needs visible

The realisation of children's rights demands a dynamic, proactive policy that anticipates situations instead of trying to deal with problems that have already arisen or emergencies. Above all, this depends on making children and their concerns visible, that is having adequate information and data on their situation, their needs and the measures required.

Whilst data are important for national policy determination and cross-country comparisons, the systematic collection of information on children is still rare in Europe. Often data, ostensibly about children, in actual fact only concern adults (for example, statistics concerning divorce do not show how many children live with their step-families). Comparative studies between countries are usually impossible because data are either not available or are incompatible owing to differences in the collection methods or definitions used. For example, differences in the definition of the concept of "custody" make it difficult to obtain an accurate picture of the deprivation of liberty applied to children, while it is difficult to assess provision for dependent children because of the wide range of definitions of the term "household". Similar problems apply in the case of child abuse, and so on.

The Council of Europe clearly has a role to play in establishing agreed definitions and collecting comparable statistical data detailed by age, gender and regions so as to identify, *inter alia*, pockets of poverty and the needs of vulnerable groups of children (minorities, refugees, etc.): to recommend that a report on the state of Europe's children be drawn up, preferably on an annual basis, setting out comprehensive details of the situation in all member states, containing a summary of positive achievements in favour of children and showing the steps still to be taken so as to comply with the requirements of the United Nations convention.

Promoting the interests of children

A proactive policy for children requires the implementation at both national and international levels of machinery to promote the interests of children as a group.

Children's affairs are traditionally the responsibility of many different ministries or central and local government departments such as education, health, justice and social services, as well as less obvious ones such as culture, finance, trade, transport or environment departments.

Not only are children's interests dispersed across these various administrative bodies, thus preventing a holistic approach to children's affairs, but individual ministries often have conflicting policies (reflected, for instance, in differences between justice and social welfare departments over the treatment of young offenders, or between trade, transport or environment and health over the prevention of accidents involving children or pollution control). Moreover, overlapping responsibilities sometimes leave gaps in child protection, which hit the most vulnerable or socially marginalised children hardest.

Steps must therefore be taken to guarantee consistency and co-ordination. In recent years, a number of European countries have become aware of the pressing need for a multidisciplinary approach. Various types of co-ordination machinery have been put in place involving, for instance, the establishment of ministries for children, interdepartmental bodies or cross-party parliamentary committees.

Spain – central government initiatives for children

In June 1989 Spain established an Inter-Ministerial Commission for Youth and Childhood, which consists of representatives from the Ministries of Social Affairs, Agriculture, Fisheries and Food,

Relations with Parliament, Culture, Foreign Affairs, Health and Consumer Affairs, Justice, Industry Trade and Tourism, Education and Science, Public Administration, Labour and Social Security, Economy and Finance, Interior, Defence and Public Works and Transport. The commission is a collegiate body, attached to the Ministry of Social Affairs, for studying the problems of youth and childhood and proposing programmes and measures that will help solve these problems, co-ordinating the activities of the various departments connected with young people and children and drawing up policies that will lead to improvements in their conditions of life. Central government is also collaborating with NGOs in subsidising programmes aimed primarily at the social inclusion of disadvantaged children, offending children and the education of children aged 0-3. At the same time it has launched through the mass media a campaign "Get to know children" based both on the need to protect children and to actively involve them and encourage their autonomy.

Germany – cross-party parliamentary structures

An official Parliamentary Commission on Children's Affairs began work in Germany in 1988. The commission consists of one Bundestag member from each of the four main political parties. Its main task is to review and influence federal laws affecting children and to promote the interests of children within the Bundestag. When the commission arrives at a consensus view its recommendations can have significant impact on the formation of policy and legislation.

Denmark – an action plan for children and young people

Denmark, in common with other countries, faces difficulties in working effectively and intersectorally on behalf of disadvantaged children. An interministerial committee from sixteen ministries, under the auspices of the government's children's committee, has now prepared a new action plan targeted at the 15% of Danish children who are disadvantaged, for example through poverty, disability, abuse or family breakdown. Multidisciplinary teams are being set up to advise teachers and welfare workers, particularly about preventive work with families, and to ensure that children and families have unified delivery of services; open-access anonymous advice services for children are being opened; research findings and practical advice is being disseminated on how families and children are best able to help themselves when under stress or in difficulties. The starting point for the action plan is that children's own resilience and capacity to cope must be strengthened through support.

Italy – a special commission on child affairs

A new Italian law has been drafted to institute a special commission on child affairs, responsible for the analysis and verification of the achievements of the government in the implementation of the United Nations Convention on the Rights of the Child. The relevant parliamentary commission has officially requested the collaboration of the Italian Unicef Committee, appointing it as the referent body for all pertinent documentation and in particular as an advisor on all matters concerning the rights of the child, as stated in the convention, especially children's right to information and freedom of thought.

Commissioners or ombudsmen

Some countries have appointed commissions or commissioners (ombudsmen) for children, having certain powers of their own and acting entirely independently. Most member states should introduce a children's ombudsman because not only does this office update legislation but is able to transmit information and knowledge of the child protection legislation to the general public, professional categories working with children and decision-makers.

Norway – a children's ombudsman

Norway established the first European statutory ombudsperson for children – the *Barneombud* – in 1981. The *Barneombud* is autonomous but has statutory powers. Its object is to "promote the interests of children *vis-à-vis* public and private authorities". The office works by recommending legal or policy changes to central and local governments and politicians; using the media; distributing information on children's rights; investigating and taking up individual cases and raising issues of principle which arise from them. It has no power to take decisions itself or revoke or alter decisions taken by the authorities, but it does have a statutory right of access to children's institutions and confidential information and records. It is consulted formally by government as a part of the consultative hearings process which Norwegian ministries conduct before legislative proposals are presented to parliament. The *Barneombud's* interventions both in government policy and in individual cases have led to significant changes in the lives of Norwegian children.

Austria – a network of ombudsmen

In Austria the *Jugendwohlfahrsgesetz* of 1989 constitutes the legal basis for the establishment of ombudsman systems for children and youth in each of the nine *Länder*. According to Section 10 of the Youth Welfare Act, it is the legal task of the ombudsman for children and youth to:

– counsel minors, persons legally responsible for a child and legal guardians in all matters relating to the position of the minor and the tasks of the person legally responsible for the child;

– assist in cases of disagreement about care and upbringing.

By establishing a total of ten ombudsman systems for children and youth at the federal level and in all the *Länder*, and by appointing a children's agent in Graz, Austria has created a comprehensive network even by international standards. The ombudsmen consider the United Nations Convention on the Rights of the Child an integral part of their work and thus also contribute to the implementation and development of children's rights in Austria.

Child impact statements

Whatever approach is adopted, any such bodies or persons must have sufficient powers to enable them to deal on a more or less equal footing with the various government departments concerned and to recommend or initiate policies which they believe would improve children's lives.

Given the often unpredictable or unexpected impact on children of much government action and legislation, all parliamentary bills and government measures, in whatever area, should be examined and assessed from the viewpoint of their effect on children. So-called "child-impact statements" may be used to determine the probable impact on children of any proposed measures. Such statements may either be included automatically in the normal political process (including budgetary policy-making) or left to the discretion of the person or body responsible for promoting and co-ordinating children's rights.

The Council of Europe's role

A permanent multidisciplinary structure, both intergovernmental and parliamentary, should be set up within the Council's existing framework and the limits of the available resources. Its purpose would be to deal on a comprehensive basis with all issues concerning children, with the participation, as active observers, of the other international organisations concerned such as the United

Nations Committee on the Rights of the Child, the European Parliament, Unicef, etc., the relevant NGOs and children themselves.

Representatives of the Social, Health and Family Affairs Committee and numerous children attended the Madrid Conference (1994) on the "Evolution of the role of children in family life: participation and negotiation". In the final recommendations, the Council of Europe was asked "in its own activities to seek to learn from the advice of children. Youth participation should be actively encouraged at conferences and other meetings, not only when child-related matters are discussed. This will require a constructive review of the language and terminology used by actors within the Council."

Rather than reporting regularly on the situation of children in Europe, this multidisciplinary structure would be responsible for defining common priorities and objectives and determining the indicators needed to assess progress achieved in implementing different aspects of children's rights. In monitoring progress, it would identify and publicise any positive initiatives taken to implement children's rights.

That structure should be a place for exchanges of views and debates dealing with issues which have particular priority in Europe, such as children without family, children of migrant or travelling families, child refugees, children in war zones, child employment, etc.

As regards child employment, legislative safeguards should be introduced or improved to prevent exploitation or injury to the child's development while encouraging the positive experience and involvement of children in the world of work. Effective strategies for bridging young people into work should exist, recognising the long-term personal and social consequences of unemployment.

One of the priorities should be the elimination of child poverty[1] across Europe and this requires the recognition of social consequences of poverty, both absolute and relative.

Co-operative arrangements should be established on world-wide issues including abduction, inter-country adoption, child pornography, child prostitution and other forms of exploitation.

Explicit recognition of children's civil and political rights

Unlike economic and social rights, civil and political rights are directly applicable upon ratification of the United Nations convention. Children's civil and political rights must therefore be explicitly recognised at national level.

Most European countries argue that, under their constitution or civil or criminal codes, children automatically enjoy these rights in the same manner as all adult citizens. But this is not enough.

In the majority of countries, children are always subject primarily to parental authority and secondly to control by other adults or authorities (for example in education). They should have their rights explicitly recognised, and legal, administrative and social machinery should be set up to ensure that these rights are implemented and respected.

Such explicit recognition must, for instance, guarantee children the right to their own name and nationality and to the preservation of their identity, the right to have their views heard and given due consideration, freedom of expression and information, freedom of thought, conscience, religion and association, protection of

---

1. See Unicef's 1993 report, *Child neglect in rich nations*.

privacy, physical integrity and a judicial system respectful of their rights to due process, which gives priority to social rehabilitation and regards custodial sentences for children as a last resort to be used only for short periods.

Six European countries respect children's right to physical integrity

Six European countries, Austria, Cyprus, Denmark, Finland, Norway and Sweden, have guaranteed children a legal right of physical integrity – in other words the right not to be hit or otherwise physically punished by parents or other adults in charge of them. This right has not led to inappropriate prosecutions of parents, nor to increased numbers of children in state care, nor to a rise in out-of-control or undisciplined children. On the contrary the evidence shows that such legal reform has led to major changes in public attitudes, the introduction of positive forms of child-rearing and a diminishment in abusive forms of discipline.

Portugal – a child-centred juvenile judicial system

Children under the age of 16 are not considered to be criminally liable for crimes they may commit and criminal penalties may not be applied to them. In particular they may not be locked up. When they offend, if family-based measures cannot be used, the children are placed in unlocked youth care centres or children's homes (of which about 400 places are available nationally). These are aimed exclusively at social rehabilitation, with active family involvement. Young people between sixteen and eighteen are subject to ordinary criminal legislation, but the Portuguese criminal code regards custody as a sentence of last resort, particularly for this age group. The numbers of imprisoned sixteen to eighteen year-olds, tried and untried, has diminished from 8,3% of this group of offenders in 1983 to 3,4% (324 young people in all).

Budgetary priority

Just as societies invest in their industrial infrastructures for instance, in order to ensure their economic development, they clearly also have a duty to invest in their children and give them budgetary priority. However, this duty is often not recognised even when countries are prospering, and the situation is worse still during periods of recession and, at present, in the case of certain countries moving towards the market economy.

The reason for these shortcomings is that usually the resources allocated for the specific needs of children are not visible. How can we tell, for example, what percentage of a budget goes on social and health services, education, cultural, sporting or recreational activities for children? Many people would be amazed to discover what a small slice of the cake they get. Sometimes political expediency and the favouring of shorter-term interests lie behind the lack of investment in children.

A European strategy for children must therefore seek to reverse this trend: governments should be asked to assess the actual level of resources allocated to children. The strategy must also recommend that these resources be made visible. They must be adequate and fair in relation to the spending on the needs of the other sections of the population, and they must under no circumstances be of a lesser amount. The resources concerned must be protected, that is "ring-fenced", to prevent their being used for any other purposes. Application of the "standstill" or "ratchet" principle would prevent them dropping below the highest level previously attained.

Investing in children means targeting objectives: priority should be given to areas where the returns are highest for the greatest number of children or for the most disadvantaged. Special budgetary resources should therefore be focused on preventive services or on services for children in their early years.

Information, education and participation

A guiding principle of this European strategy is that children's views should be heard and that children should take an active part in decision-making which affects them. This should occur at every level of society and in every sort of decision-making.

Scandinavian measures to ensure that children's views are respected within the family

Under a 1983 act, before making a decision on a matter affecting a child, Finnish parents and custodians are under a statutory duty to "where possible, discuss the matter with the child taking into account the child's age and maturity and the nature of the matter. In making the decision the custodian shall give due consideration to the child's feelings, opinions and wishes." A 1981 Norwegian act similarly requires parents to hear the views of the child on relevant decisions, and in Sweden custodians must "in step with the child's advancing age and development, make increasing allowance for the child's views and wishes".

France – representing children's views in towns, schools and institutions

Over the last fifteen years more than 700 towns in France have developed children's councils. Children aged between nine and eighteen are elected by their peers to represent children's views, over a two-year period, to elected members and local decision-makers, in partnership with teachers, town-planners and local organisations. The effective advocacy of these young representatives has led to real changes in the lives of local children – for example in urban planning, increased play spaces, cheap access to cultural events, healthier environments, safer traffic routes and measures to combat racism and drug abuse. In education, not only schools have student councils, but also every educational district has student representation and at national level three high school pupils are elected (and trained) to sit on the Central Board of Education and take part in the major discussions on the educational system. By law children over twelve years of age living in social or medical institutions must be involved, with their parents, in the operation of the institution including participation in the board of administration.

Poland – children's rights in schools

Poland's 1991 Education Act entitles pupils to rights of representation on all school matters; pupils' representatives are also allowed to participate in the school committees which are responsible for solving internal school problems. Teachers are required to be guided by the pupils' interests, concern for their health and the principle of respect for the personal dignity of each pupil. Poland was the first European country to ban corporal punishment in schools – in 1783. A number of areas have instituted an ombudsman for pupils' rights (as yet on a non-statutory basis) as a measure to prevent and solve school conflicts. Initial evaluation suggests that these ombudsmen are more effective than administrative or legal interventions.

Information for children, dialogue, the sharing of decision-making and the non-violent resolution of conflicts are essential elements in teaching children to play a responsible part in family life, defined as the smallest democracy at the heart of society, and even more so in society itself.

Such active involvement of children must extend to other areas like schools, hospitals and children's homes. In some countries, children are already involved in running various institutions of this kind, for instance through seats on governing boards. We must promote dialogue between children and various professionals, policy-makers and judicial or administrative authorities.

Children's councils or children's elected representatives can work together with adult councillors and defend and promote children's interests. They make significant contributions in areas such as urban planning, traffic problems, measures to combat racism, drug abuse or juvenile crime. In some cases, the members of certain professions are required by national legislation or their own professional codes of practice to seek children's views and give them due attention.

Realising children's rights means informing children about these rights. The information provided must also cover the legal and other remedies available to children if, for example, they suffer abuse. Some countries have developed a free telephone service where children can talk in confidence and seek assistance. Specific training on children's rights must also be given to all professionals who come into contact with children.

The Netherlands – children's easy access to help, advice and advocacy

Advice centres for young people (the JAB: *jongeren adviesburo*) were set up almost thirty years ago by local social services departments. These advise young people between the ages of 12 and 25 on areas such as education, health care, housing and employment. They can come on their own or with a parent or friend. Despite the high demand for this service there are no waiting lists as the aim is to solve problems as quickly as possible. If longer-term help is needed the JAB will offer advocacy and mediation, visiting families, accompanying the young person to meetings and offering group therapy. The service is widely advertised through schools and youth clubs.

Children's education rights should be developed, such as access to free education for the pre-school, primary and secondary range; free special education provisions; systematic development of integrated education (both in terms of disability and across cultural/religious divisions). Development of the curriculum and school structures should be in line with the United Nations convention and Council of Europe goals for education. Teaching the rights and responsibilities of children should already be included in the curriculum at primary school level.

Through schools and also via the media – foremost among which, due to its impact, the television – countries should also take steps to give education wider aims,[1] such as teaching children to prevent racism,[2] to show tolerance and goodwill towards people from different backgrounds, education for peace and non-violent conflict resolution, health education (including sex education, drug education and education for parenthood) and, of course, education for citizenship. Above all, children must be educated to become responsible citizens who understand and subscribe to the values of the democratic society in which they live and ought to play an active part.

Solidarity and Europe's responsibilities

Our continent of Europe does not exist in isolation from the rest of the world. However, this obvious truth, which is readily accepted,

---

1. A recent education act in Spain establishes some issues that must be addressed throughout the different curricula subjects. These include moral and civic education, education for peace, education for health, education for equality of opportunity for the two sexes, environmental education, sex education, consumer education and education on traffic rules.
2. On 28 June 1995 the Social, Health and Family Affairs Committee held an exchange of views with Professor Magne Raundalen of the Crisis Psychology Centre at the University of Bergen (Norway), who expressed his conviction that racism and xenophobia could be prevented in childhood, during what he termed the golden age, that is between the ages of 8 and 12 ; schools must be made responsible for giving children positive attitudes, and the right kind of environment must also be developed outside through awareness-raising and by involving civil society and the media.

not to say worshipped, in the business sector, meets with much self-interest and reticence when it comes to discussing human beings and the possible and desirable forms of interdependence and solidarity between Europe and the rest of the planet.

Yet the lives and fates of children in countries which are not members of the Council of Europe are very often greatly influenced by the activities of European countries, whether governments, companies or individuals. That is why our commitment to the rights of children helps countries throughout the world. We only need mention the economic exploitation of children or the forced child labour found in certain developing countries, the exploitation of young girls and boys by European "sex tourists", and children who are the victims of war, left starving, or disabled for life by weapons such as land mines produced and exported by European countries.

The prevarications of the international community over the possible introduction of a social clause in international trade relations or the banning of certain types of weapon are deplorable. Some countries happily do not hesitate in departing somewhat from their traditional rules of law to combat acts of child abuse more efficiently at international level, for example by ensuring that their citizens be prosecuted in case of offences committed abroad.[1]

If they are to be credible, our efforts to promote children's rights must be consistent. Europe, as a continent favoured by a high level of industrialisation and wealth, must assume its responsibility for the world's needy children.

---

1. For example, the Belgian law of 13 April 1995 on the suppression of the slave trade in human beings and of child pornography stipulates, in its Chapter III, Article 8, that any Belgian citizen, or foreigner in Belgium, can be prosecuted, even in the absence of a complaint or official notification from a foreign authority, in the event of offences committed outside the territory of the kingdom against minors less than 16 years old.

Europe must therefore commit itself to implement effectively and universally the provisions of the United Nations Convention on Children's Rights. As an aid donor, it must commit itself to increasing its aid to at least 0,7% of GNP and devoting at least 20% of its aid to basic social services for human development and show far more sympathy to poor and third world countries on the policies of repayment of debts caused by the borrowing of funds from world aid organisations.

Conclusions

This strategy, which is meant to help advance the cause of the rights of the child should give rise to a number of recommendations to be addressed to the states grouped together in the Council of Europe and to the Organisation itself. The states should be asked to:

– reaffirm their attachment to certain fundamental principles and, if this has not yet been done, to ratify and implement the United Nations Convention on the Rights of the Child without reservations, as well as the different relevant conventions of the Council of Europe;

– demonstrate their political will to help promote this cause at national level, through the adoption of a proactive policy in favour of the child implying, *inter alia*: the setting up of political and administrative structures capable of promoting the rights and interests of children; guaranteed appropriate budgetary allocations; an explicit recognition of the civil and political rights of the child.

At international level states should be asked to continue, and indeed increase, their development aid, and to intensify international co-operation and co-ordination, in particular at European level.

The Council of Europe, as the guardian of human rights, has a specific role to play in promoting the cause of children and placing children's rights among the fundamental values of European civilisations.

Conclusion

Adults have long tended to see children as isolated beings still undergoing development, (a "not-yet" human being). Today, a new view of the child is emerging. Children are human beings with their own rights and responsibilities, and want to be able to take an active part in family and social life.

Children are citizens of present-day society, to which they make their own contribution. They are tomorrow's adults. They are not only biologically valuable, but also help to maintain social organisation and transmit cultural values. Adult society has an undeniable interest (and not only an economic one) in investing in the next generation.

Nobody today would dream of denying the state's responsibility towards all citizens, and it therefore must shoulder its long-term responsibility towards children. Their vulnerability, exacerbated by a lack of involvement in society, only serves to increase the state's responsibility towards them.

Our societies have weighed down the next generation with a burden which is hard to bear, including high levels of debt, the destruction and pollution of the environment and conflicts arising from racism and intolerance, etc. Talking about children's rights also means considering the kind of society we shall bequeath to them.

Children are one of the largest groups in society. Unlike other groups (for example the elderly), however, they do not form a lobby and, as they are not entitled to vote, few politicians take up the defense of their interests in the competition for resources. Children are usually absent from political life and, in particular, are forgotten when it comes to decisions on allocating funds. At every level of the decision-making process, they are rarely represented.

In order to improve their situation, children as citizens must be made more visible in society, and a multidisciplinary approach must be adopted, modelled on that taken in most countries for women's causes, which undoubtedly has helped to bring about greater equality between the sexes.

After fighting the differences between the sexes, we must set about eliminating unjustified differences between the generations, as well as fostering democracy and greater equality between adults and children.

Promoting a pact between the generations is particularly necessary in view of the inverse pyramid of the ages and the increasing and large number of retired people for whom the future generations will be responsible.

We should never forget the basic need of children such as food, shelter, clothing, adequate medical treatment and – last but certainly not least – loving warmth and care.

A child should be able to enjoy the right to play, to experiment and discover, the right to have time for his or herself and to meet with other children without being overburdened with duties and obligations and without being unduly exposed to the dangers of modern society whether they be sexual abuse, drugs, motor traffic, child labour or, simply, cruelty at home.

Above all a child should be able to enjoy the right to a childhood.

Appendix

Recommendation 1286[1]
on a European strategy for children

1.   In its Resolution 1011 (1993) on the situation of women and children in the former Yugoslavia, the Assembly urged all the states grouped together in the Council of Europe to subscribe to the principle of "first call for children", to recognise children's rights, their universality and indivisibility and to provide for their essential needs both in Europe and in the rest of the world.

2.   The Assembly decided in Order No. 491 (1993) to develop, in co-operation with Unicef, a strategy for children up to the age of eighteen which at European level could serve as inspiration and guidance for policy-makers and all those who actively support children's causes in their respective activities. It would like to pay particular tribute to Unicef, without whose experience and expertise such a strategy would not have been possible.

3.   The Assembly notes that the rights of the child are still far from being a reality in our own rich and developed continent of Europe and that children are often the first victims of armed conflicts, economic recession, poverty, and in particular budgetary constraints.

4.   Accordingly, it is important for the Assembly that states should be helped to give effect, within their own national situation, to the commitments entered into under the United Nations Convention on the Rights of

---

1. Assembly debate on 24 January 1996 (4th Sitting) (see Doc. 7436, report of the Social, Health and Family Affairs Committee, rapporteur: Mr Cox; and Doc. 7473, opinion of the Committee on Legal Affairs and Human Rights, rapporteur: Mrs Err).
   Text adopted by the Assembly on 24 January 1996 (4th Sitting).

the Child, to promote a change in the way children, as individuals with rights, are viewed and also to encourage their active and responsible participation within the family and society.

5.   Children are citizens of the society of today and tomorrow. Society has a long-term responsibility to support children and has to acknowledge the rights of the family in the interest of the child. Responding to children's rights, interests and needs must be a political priority. The Assembly is convinced that respect for children's rights and greater equality between children and adults will help preserve the pact between generations and will contribute towards democracy.

6.   The Assembly recommends that the Committee of Ministers urge the member states of the Council of Europe:

   i.   to ratify the United Nations Convention on the Rights of the Child if they have not already done so, to withdraw any reservations made and to implement the convention in the letter and the spirit by reviewing and adapting their legislative and regulatory provisions;

   ii.   to ratify all the relevant Council of Europe conventions on the rights and protection of the child, in particular the recent European Convention on the Exercise of Children's Rights.

7.   The Assembly also recommends that the Committee of Ministers invite the states grouped together in the Council of Europe to make children's rights a political priority by:

   i.   adopting at national and local level a proactive childhood policy which seeks full implementation of the Convention on the Rights of the Child, which will consider the best interests of the child as a guiding principle of all action and which will anticipate situations instead of trying to deal with emergencies or problems that have already arisen;

   ii.   making children more visible through the systematic collection of information, in particular reliable, detailed (by age and gender), comparable statistics which will make it possible to identify their needs and the issues which require priority political action;

   iii.   adopting a comprehensive, consistent and co-ordinated approach to childhood policy, which will encourage multidisciplinary structures to be put in place at all deliberation and decision-making levels, in particular at ministerial level, and foster the creation of national coalitions of all relevant partners;

iv. appointing a commissioner (ombudsman) for children or another structure offering guarantees of independence, and the responsibilities required to improve children's lives, and accessible to the public through such means as local offices;

v. ensuring, especially at policy-making level, that the interests and needs of children are always duly considered and taken into account, for example by introducing practices such as the "child impact statement" which offers a way of determining the probable impact on children of any proposed legislative, regulatory or other measures in whatever field, for example, in the field of legal aid;

vi. investing in children and giving them budgetary priority by allocating adequate and fair resources in relation to spending on the needs of the other sections of the population at all levels (national, regional, local);

vii. guaranteeing the present level of their contributions and subsidies to the various national and international organisations involved in child care.

8. The Committee of Ministers should strongly urge these states:

i. to guarantee, through explicit recognition in their constitutional texts or domestic law, children's civil and political rights, as well as their economic, social and cultural rights, as enshrined in the United Nations Convention on the Rights of the Child;

ii. to guarantee to all children the right to free and high quality education for pre-school, primary and secondary education;

iii. to inform children and also their parents of their rights by widely publicising and disseminating the text of the Convention on the Rights of the Child, by all possible means, including the use of the media and by introducing education on children's rights and responsibilities into the school curriculum from primary level onwards;

iv. to encourage the media, notably visual, to promote children's right to a healthy and balanced development, and in particular in products intended for children, to eliminate violence and to illustrate positive social values;

v. to inform children about the means and remedies available to them in the event of violation of their fundamental rights and, for example, to extend the provision of free help-lines, specialist advocates and child friendly judicial and administrative systems which recognise the claims of individual children for protection against all forms of abuse;

vi. to provide specific training in children's rights for all professionals who come into contact with children, including teachers, the various members of the judicial authorities, social workers, etc.;

vii. to enable the views of children to be heard in all decision-making which affects them, and to enable them to participate actively, responsibly and in a manner appropriate to their capacity, at all levels of society – in the family, in local communities, in schools and other institutions, in judicial hearings and in national government;

viii. to teach children how to act as responsible citizens, to encourage them to take an interest in public affairs and to reconsider the age at which young people can vote;

ix. to promote education for the prevention of racism, political and religious intolerance and violence and for the learning of tolerance and peaceful resolution of conflict;

x. to pay particular attention to the situation and the specific needs of immigrant and refugee children and minority and marginalised children;

xi. to emphasise to parents, families, teachers and all those involved directly or indirectly with children, as they develop into adulthood, that in a civilised society responsibilities and obligations go hand in hand with rights and privileges.

9. The Assembly also recommends that the Committee of Ministers invite these states to give credibility and consistency to the debate on children's rights by making it a reality outside Europe by:

i. making a commitment to work towards ensuring that the provisions of the Convention on the Rights of the Child are upheld throughout the world, via all appropriate unilateral or multilateral measures to combat the exploitation of children and to protect them from the effects of armed conflicts;

ii. promoting international co-operation and in particular by increasing their aid to the developing countries to at least 0,7% of GNP and devoting at least 20% of their aid to basic social services which are indispensable for human development;

iii. adopting a more understanding common attitude to the repayment by these countries of the debt incurred with the international development aid organisations.

10. Finally, the Assembly recommends that the Committee of Ministers:

i. set up, within the Council of Europe, a permanent multidisciplinary intergovernmental structure able to deal with all issues relating to children;

ii. instruct it, as part of its terms of reference, to draw up an annual report on the state of Europe's children, giving a comprehensive account of the situation and an outline of positive achievements and serving as a measure of what else needs to be done to satisfy the requirements of the Convention on the Rights of the Child, and to submit this report to the Parliamentary Assembly; this report will be the subject of an annual discussion within the relevant Parliamentary Assembly committee;

iii. involve other competent international organisations, in particular the United Nations Committee on the Rights of the Child, the European Parliament, Unicef, the various relevant non-governmental organisations, and indeed children themselves in the activities of this structure in the appropriate forms;

iv. transmit the present recommendation to states grouped in the Council of Europe, to the aforementioned organisations and to the closing conference of the Multidisciplinary Project on Childhood Policies to be held in Leipzig in spring 1996.

European Convention on the Exercise of Children's Rights[1]

Preamble

The member States of the Council of Europe and the other States signatory hereto,

Considering that the aim of the Council of Europe is to achieve greater unity between its members;

Having regard to the United Nations Convention on the Rights of the Child and in particular Article 4 which requires States Parties to undertake all appropriate legislative, administrative and other measures for the implementation of the rights recognised in the said Convention;

Noting the contents of Recommendation 1121 (1990) of the Parliamentary Assembly on the rights of the child;

Convinced that the rights and best interests of children should be promoted and to that end children should have the opportunity to exercise their rights, in particular in family proceedings affecting them;

Recognising that children should be provided with relevant information to enable such rights and best interests to be promoted and that due weight should be given to the views of children;

Recognising the importance of the parental role in protecting and promoting the rights and best interests of children and considering

---

1. European Treaty Series, No. 160. Convention entered into force on 25 January 1996.

that, where necessary, states should also engage in such protection and promotion;

Considering, however, that in the event of conflict it is desirable for families to try to reach agreement before bringing the matter before a judicial authority,

Have agreed as follows:

Chapter I – Scope and object of the Convention and definitions

Article 1 – Scope and object of the Convention

1 This Convention shall apply to children who have not reached the age of 18 years.

2 The object of the present Convention is, in the best interests of children, to promote their rights, to grant them procedural rights and to facilitate the exercise of these rights by ensuring that children are, themselves or through other persons or bodies, informed and allowed to participate in proceedings affecting them before a judicial authority.

3 For the purposes of this Convention proceedings before a judicial authority affecting children are family proceedings, in particular those involving the exercise of parental responsibilities such as residence and access to children.

4 Every State shall, at the time of signature or when depositing its instrument of ratification, acceptance, approval or accession, by a declaration addressed to the Secretary General of the Council of Europe, specify at least three categories of family cases before a judicial authority to which this Convention is to apply.

5 Any Party may, by further declaration, specify additional categories of family cases to which this Convention is to apply or provide information concerning the application of Article 5, paragraph 2 of Article 9, paragraph 2 of Article 10 and Article 11.

6 Nothing in this Convention shall prevent Parties from applying

rules more favourable to the promotion and the exercise of children's rights.

Article 2 – Definitions

For the purposes of this Convention:

a   the term "judicial authority" means a court or an administrative authority having equivalent powers;

b   the term "holders of parental responsibilities" means parents and other persons or bodies entitled to exercise some or all parental responsibilities;

c   the term "representative" means a person, such as a lawyer, or a body appointed to act before a judicial authority on behalf of a child;

d   the term "relevant information" means information which is appropriate to the age and understanding of the child, and which will be given to enable the child to exercise his or her rights fully unless the provision of such information were contrary to the welfare of the child.

Chapter II – Procedural measures to promote the exercise of children's rights

A. Procedural rights of a child

Article 3 – Right to be informed and to express his or her views in proceedings

A child considered by internal law as having sufficient understanding, in the case of proceedings before a judicial authority affecting him or her, shall be granted, and shall be entitled to request, the following rights:

a   to receive all relevant information;

b   to be consulted and express his or her views;

c   to be informed of the possible consequences of compliance with these views and the possible consequences of any decision.

Article 4 – Right to apply for the appointment of a special representative

1 Subject to Article 9, the child shall have the right to apply, in person or through other persons or bodies, for a special representative in proceedings before a judicial authority affecting the child where internal law precludes the holders of parental responsibilities from representing the child as a result of a conflict of interest with the latter.

2 States are free to limit the right in paragraph 1 to children who are considered by internal law to have sufficient understanding.

Article 5 – Other possible procedural rights

Parties shall consider granting children additional procedural rights in relation to proceedings before a judicial authority affecting them, in particular:

a the right to apply to be assisted by an appropriate person of their choice in order to help them express their views;

b the right to apply themselves, or through other persons or bodies, for the appointment of a separate representative, in appropriate cases a lawyer;

c the right to appoint their own representative;

d the right to exercise some or all of the rights of parties to such proceedings.

B. Role of judicial authorities

Article 6 – Decision-making process

In proceedings affecting a child, the judicial authority, before taking a decision, shall:

a consider whether it has sufficient information at its disposal in order to take a decision in the best interests of the child and, where necessary, it shall obtain further information, in particular from the holders of parental responsibilities;

b in a case where the child is considered by internal law as having sufficient understanding:

  – ensure that the child has received all relevant information;

  – consult the child in person in appropriate cases, if necessary privately, itself or through other persons or bodies, in a manner appropriate to his or her understanding, unless this would be manifestly contrary to the best interests of the child;

  – allow the child to express his or her views;

c give due weight to the views expressed by the child.

Article 7 – Duty to act speedily

In proceedings affecting a child the judicial authority shall act speedily to avoid any unnecessary delay and procedures shall be available to ensure that its decisions are rapidly enforced. In urgent cases the judicial authority shall have the power, where appropriate, to take decisions which are immediately enforceable.

Article 8 – Acting on own motion

In proceedings affecting a child the judicial authority shall have the power to act on its own motion in cases determined by internal law where the welfare of a child is in serious danger.

Article 9 – Appointment of a representative

1 In proceedings affecting a child where, by internal law, the holders of parental responsibilities are precluded from representing the child as a result of a conflict of interest between them and the child, the judicial authority shall have the power to appoint a special representative for the child in those proceedings.

2 Parties shall consider providing that, in proceedings affecting a child, the judicial authority shall have the power to appoint a separate representative, in appropriate cases a lawyer, to represent the child.

C. Role of representatives

Article 10

1 In the case of proceedings before a judicial authority affecting a child the representative shall, unless this would be manifestly contrary to the best interests of the child:

   a provide all relevant information to the child, if the child is considered by internal law as having sufficient understanding;

   b provide explanations to the child if the child is considered by internal law as having sufficient understanding, concerning the possible consequences of compliance with his or her views and the possible consequences of any action by the representative;

   c determine the views of the child and present these views to the judicial authority.

2 Parties shall consider extending the provisions of paragraph 1 to the holders of parental responsibilities.

D. Extension of certain provisions

Article 11

Parties shall consider extending the provisions of Articles 3, 4 and 9 to proceedings affecting children before other bodies and to matters affecting children which are not the subject of proceedings.

E. National bodies

Article 12

1 Parties shall encourage, through bodies which perform, *inter alia*, the functions set out in paragraph 2, the promotion and the exercise of children's rights.

2 The functions are as follows:

   a to make proposals to strengthen the law relating to the exercise of children's rights;

b to give opinions concerning draft legislation relating to the exercise of children's rights;

c to provide general information concerning the exercise of children's rights to the media, the public and persons and bodies dealing with questions relating to children;

d to seek the views of children and provide them with relevant information.

F. Other matters

Article 13 – Mediation or other processes to resolve disputes

In order to prevent or resolve disputes or to avoid proceedings before a judicial authority affecting children, Parties shall encourage the provision of mediation or other processes to resolve disputes and the use of such processes to reach agreement in appropriate cases to be determined by Parties.

Article 14 – Legal aid and advice

Where internal law provides for legal aid or advice for the representation of children in proceedings before a judicial authority affecting them, such provisions shall apply in relation to the matters covered by Articles 4 and 9.

Article 15 – Relations with other international instruments

This Convention shall not restrict the application of any other international instrument which deals with specific issues arising in the context of the protection of children and families, and to which a Party to this Convention is, or becomes, a Party.

Chapter III – Standing Committee

Article 16 – Establishment and functions of the Standing Committee

1 A Standing Committee is set up for the purposes of this Convention.

2 The Standing Committee shall keep under review problems relating to this Convention. It may, in particular:

   a consider any relevant questions concerning the interpretation or implementation of the Convention. The Standing Committee's conclusions concerning the implementation of the Convention may take the form of a recommendation; recommendations shall be adopted by a three-quarters majority of the votes cast;

   b propose amendments to the Convention and examine those proposed in accordance with Article 20;

   c provide advice and assistance to the national bodies having the functions under paragraph 2 of Article 12 and promote international co-operation between them.

Article 17 – Composition

1 Each Party may be represented on the Standing Committee by one or more delegates. Each Party shall have one vote.

2 Any State referred to in Article 21, which is not a Party to this Convention, may be represented in the Standing Committee by an observer. The same applies to any other State or to the European Community after having been invited to accede to the Convention in accordance with the provisions of Article 22.

3 Unless a Party has informed the Secretary General of its objection at least one month before the meeting, the Standing Committee may invite the following to attend as observers at all its meetings or at one meeting or part of a meeting:

   - any State not referred to in paragraph 2 above;

   - the United Nations Committee on the Rights of the Child;

   - the European Community;

   - any international governmental body;

   - any international non-governmental body with one or more functions mentioned under paragraph 2 of Article 12;

- any national governmental or non-governmental body with one or more functions mentioned under paragraph 2 of Article 12.

4 The Standing Committee may exchange information with relevant organisations dealing with the exercise of children's rights.

Article 18 – Meetings

1 At the end of the third year following the date of entry into force of this Convention and, on his or her own initiative, at any time after this date, the Secretary General of the Council of Europe shall invite the Standing Committee to meet.

2 Decisions may only be taken in the Standing Committee if at least one-half of the Parties are present.

3 Subject to Articles 16 and 20 the decisions of the Standing Committee shall be taken by a majority of the members present.

4 Subject to the provisions of this Convention the Standing Committee shall draw up its own rules of procedure and the rules of procedure of any working party it may set up to carry out all appropriate tasks under the Convention.

Article 19 – Reports of the Standing Committee

After each meeting, the Standing Committee shall forward to the Parties and the Committee of Ministers of the Council of Europe a report on its discussions and any decisions taken.

Chapter IV – Amendments to the Convention

Article 20

1 Any amendment to the articles of this Convention proposed by a Party or the Standing Committee shall be communicated to the Secretary General of the Council of Europe and forwarded by him or her, at least two months before the next meeting of the Standing Committee, to the member States of the Council of Europe,

any signatory, any Party, any State invited to sign this Convention in accordance with the provisions of Article 21 and any State or the European Community invited to accede to it in accordance with the provisions of Article 22.

2 Any amendment proposed in accordance with the provisions of the preceding paragraph shall be examined by the Standing Committee which shall submit the text adopted by a three-quarters majority of the votes cast to the Committee of Ministers for approval. After its approval, this text shall be forwarded to the Parties for acceptance.

3 Any amendment shall enter into force on the first day of the month following the expiration of a period of one month after the date on which all Parties have informed the Secretary General that they have accepted it.

Chapter V – Final clauses

Article 21 – Signature, ratification and entry into force

1 This Convention shall be open for signature by the member States of the Council of Europe and the non-member States which have participated in its elaboration.

2 This Convention is subject to ratification, acceptance or approval. Instruments of ratification, acceptance or approval shall be deposited with the Secretary General of the Council of Europe.

3 This Convention shall enter into force on the first day of the month following the expiration of a period of three months after the date on which three States, including at least two member States of the Council of Europe, have expressed their consent to be bound by the Convention in accordance with the provisions of the preceding paragraph.

4 In respect of any signatory which subsequently expresses its consent to be bound by it, the Convention shall enter into force on the first day of the month following the expiration of a period

of three months after the date of the deposit of its instrument of ratification, acceptance or approval.

Article 22 – Non-member States and the European Community

1 After the entry into force of this Convention, the Committee of Ministers of the Council of Europe may, on its own initiative or following a proposal from the Standing Committee and after consultation of the Parties, invite any non-member State of the Council of Europe, which has not participated in the elaboration of the Convention, as well as the European Community to accede to this Convention by a decision taken by the majority provided for in Article 20, sub-paragraph d of the Statute of the Council of Europe, and by the unanimous vote of the representatives of the contracting States entitled to sit on the Committee of Ministers.

2 In respect of any acceding State or the European Community, the Convention shall enter into force on the first day of the month following the expiration of a period of three months after the date of deposit of the instrument of accession with the Secretary General of the Council of Europe.

Article 23 – Territorial application

1 Any State may, at the time of signature or when depositing its instrument of ratification, acceptance, approval or accession, specify the territory or territories to which this Convention shall apply.

2 Any Party may, at any later date, by a declaration addressed to the Secretary General of the Council of Europe, extend the application of this Convention to any other territory specified in the declaration and for whose international relations it is responsible or on whose behalf it is authorised to give undertakings. In respect of such territory the Convention shall enter into force on the first day of the month following the expiration of a period of three months after the date of receipt of such declaration by the Secretary General.

3 Any declaration made under the two preceding paragraphs may, in respect of any territory specified in such declaration, be withdrawn by a notification addressed to the Secretary General. The withdrawal shall become effective on the first day of the month following the expiration of a period of three months after the date of receipt of such notification by the Secretary General.

Article 24 – Reservations

No reservation may be made to the Convention.

Article 25 – Denunciation

1 Any Party may at any time denounce this Convention by means of a notification addressed to the Secretary General of the Council of Europe.

2 Such denunciation shall become effective on the first day of the month following the expiration of a period of three months after the date of receipt of notification by the Secretary General.

Article 26 – Notifications

The Secretary General of the Council of Europe shall notify the member States of the Council, any signatory, any Party and any other State or the European Community which has been invited to accede to this Convention of:

a any signature;

b the deposit of any instrument of ratification, acceptance, approval or accession;

c any date of entry into force of this Convention in accordance with Articles 21 or 22;

d any amendment adopted in accordance with Article 20 and the date on which such an amendment enters into force;

e any declaration made under the provisions of Articles 1 and 23;

f   any denunciation made in pursuance of the provisions of Article 25 ;

g   any other act, notification or communication relating to this Convention.

In witness whereof, the undersigned, being duly authorised thereto, have signed this Convention.

Done at Strasbourg, this 25th Day of January 1996, in English and French, both texts being equally authentic, in a single copy which shall be deposited in the archives of the Council of Europe. The Secretary General of the Council of Europe shall transmit certified copies to each member State of the Council of Europe, to the non-member States which have participated in the elaboration of this Convention, to the European Community and to any State invited to accede to this Convention.

United Nations Convention on the Rights of the Child

PREAMBLE

The States Parties to the present Convention,

Considering that, in accordance with the principles proclaimed in the Charter of the United Nations, recognition of the inherent dignity and of the equal and inalienable rights of all members of the human family is the foundation of freedom, justice and peace in the world,

Bearing in mind that the peoples of the United Nations have, in the Charter, reaffirmed their faith in fundamental human rights and in the dignity and worth of the human person, and have determined to promote social progress and better standards of life in larger freedom,

Recognizing that the United Nations has, in the Universal Declaration of Human Rights and in the International Covenants on Human Rights, proclaimed and agreed that everyone is entitled to all the rights and freedoms set forth therein, without distinction of any kind, such as race, colour, sex, language, religion, political or other opinion, national or social origin, property, birth or other status,

Recalling that, in the Universal Declaration of Human Rights, the United Nations has proclaimed that childhood is entitled to special care and assistance,

Convinced that the family, as the fundamental group of society and the natural environment for the growth and well-being of all its members and

---

1. Adopted by the General Assembly of the United Nations on 20 November 1989.

particularly children, should be afforded the necessary protection and assistance so that it can fully assume its responsibilities within the community,

Recognizing that the child, for the full and harmonious development of his or her personality, should grow up in a family environment, in an atmosphere of happiness, love and understanding,

Considering that the child should be fully prepared to live an individual life in society, and brought up in the spirit of the ideals proclaimed in the Charter of the United Nations, and in particular in the spirit of peace, dignity, tolerance, freedom, equality and solidarity,

Bearing in mind that the need to extend particular care to the child has been stated in the Geneva Declaration of the Rights of the Child of 1924 and in the Declaration of the Rights of the Child adopted by the United Nations on 20 November 1959 and recognized in the Universal Declaration of Human Rights, in the International Covenant on Civil and Political Rights (in particular in articles 23 and 24), in the International Covenant on Economic, Social and Cultural Rights (in particular in article 10) and in the statutes and relevant instruments of specialized agencies and international organizations concerned with the welfare of children,

Bearing in mind that, as indicated in the Declaration of the Rights of the Child, "the child, by reason of his physical and mental immaturity, needs special safeguards and care, including appropriate legal protection, before as well as after birth",

Recalling the provisions of the Declaration on Social and Legal Principles relating to the Protection and Welfare of Children, with Special Reference to Foster Placement and Adoption Nationally and Internationally; the United Nations Standard Minimum Rules for the Administration of Juvenile Justice ("The Beijing Rules"); and the Declaration on the Protection of Women and Children in Emergency and Armed Conflict,

Recognizing that, in all countries in the world, there are children living in exceptionally difficult conditions, and that such children need special consideration,

Taking due account of the importance of the traditions and cultural values of each people for the protection and harmonious development of the child,

Recognizing the importance of international co-operation for improving the living conditions of children in every country, in particular in the developing countries,

Have agreed as follows:

Part I

Article 1

For the purposes of the present Convention, a child means every human being below the age of 18 years unless, under the law applicable to the child, majority is attained earlier.

Article 2

1.   States Parties shall respect and ensure the rights set forth in the present Convention to each child within their jurisdiction without discrimination of any kind, irrespective of the child's or his or her parent's or legal guardian's race, colour, sex, language, religion, political or other opinion, national, ethnic or social origin, property, disability, birth or other status.

2.   States Parties shall take all appropriate measures to ensure that the child is protected against all forms of discrimination or punishment on the basis of the status, activities, expressed opinions, or beliefs of the child's parents, legal guardians, or family members.

Article 3

1.   In all actions concerning children, whether undertaken by public or private social welfare institutions, courts of law, administrative authorities or legislative bodies, the best interests of the child shall be a primary consideration.

2.   States Parties undertake to ensure the child such protection and care as is necessary for his or her well-being, taking into account the rights and duties of his or her parents, legal guardians, or other individuals legally responsible for him or her, and, to this end, shall take all appropriate legislative and administrative measures.

3.   States Parties shall ensure that the institutions, services and facilities responsible for the care or protection of children shall conform with the standards established by competent authorities, particularly in the areas of safety, health, in the number and suitability of their staff, as well as competent supervision.

Article 4

States Parties shall undertake all appropriate legislative, administrative, and other measures for the implementation of the rights recognized in the present Convention. With regard to economic, social and cultural rights, States Parties shall undertake such measures to the maximum extent of their available resources and, where needed, within the framework of international co-operation.

Article 5

States Parties shall respect the responsibilities, rights and duties of parents or, where applicable, the members of the extended family or community as provided for by   local custom, legal guardians or other persons legally responsible for the child, to provide, in a manner consistent with the evolving capacities of the child, appropriate direction and guidance in the exercise by the child of the rights recognized in the present Convention.

Article 6

1.   States Parties recognize that every child has the inherent right to life.

2.   States Parties shall ensure to the maximum extent possible the survival and development of the child.

Article 7

1.   The child shall be registered immediately after birth and shall have the right from birth to a name, the right to acquire a nationality and, as far as possible, the right to know and be cared for by his or her parents.

2.   States Parties shall ensure the implementation of these rights in accordance with their national law and their obligations under the relevant international instruments in this field, in particular where the child would otherwise be stateless.

Article 8

1.   States Parties undertake to respect the right of the child to preserve his or her identity, including nationality, name and family relations as recognized by law without unlawful interference.

2.   Where a child is illegally deprived of some or all of the elements of his or her identity, States Parties shall provide appropriate assistance and protection, with a view to speedily re-establishing his or her identity.

Article 9

1.   States Parties shall ensure that a child shall not be separated from his or her parents against their will, except when competent authorities subject to judicial review determine, in accordance with applicable law and procedures, that such separation is necessary for the best interests of the child. Such determination may be necessary in a particular case such as one involving abuse or neglect of the child by the parents, or one where the parents are living separately and a decision must be made as to the child's place of residence.

2.   In any proceedings pursuant to paragraph 1 of the present article, all interested parties shall be given an opportunity to participate in the proceedings and make their views known.

3.   States Parties shall respect the right of the child who is separated from one or both parents to maintain personal relations and direct contact with

both parents on a regular basis, except if it is contrary to the child's best interests.

4. Where such separation results from any action initiated by a State Party, such as the detention, imprisonment, exile, deportation or death (including death arising from any cause while the person is in the custody of the State) of one or both parents or of the child, that State Party shall, upon request, provide the parents, the child or, if appropriate, another member of the family with the essential information concerning the whereabouts of the absent member(s) of the family unless the provision of the information would be detrimental to the well-being of the child. States Parties shall further ensure that the submission of such a request shall of itself entail no adverse consequences for the person(s) concerned.

Article 10

1. In accordance with the obligation of States Parties under article 9, paragraph 1, applications by a child or his or her parents to enter or leave a State Party for the purpose of family reunification shall be dealt with by States Parties in a positive, humane and expeditious manner. States Parties shall further ensure that the submission of such a request shall entail no adverse consequences for the applicants and for the members of their family.

2. A child whose parents reside in different States shall have the right to maintain on a regular basis, save in exceptional circumstances personal relations and direct contacts with both parents. Towards that end and in accordance with the obligation of States Parties under article 9, paragraph 1, States Parties shall respect the right of the child and his or her parents to leave any country, including their own, and to enter their own country. The right to leave any country shall be subject only to such restrictions as are prescribed by law and which are necessary to protect the national security, public order (*ordre public*), public health or morals or the rights and freedoms of others and are consistent with the other rights recognized in the present Convention.

Article 11

1. States Parties shall take measures to combat the illicit transfer and non-return of children abroad.

2. To this end, States Parties shall promote the conclusion of bilateral or multilateral agreements or accession to existing agreements.

Article 12

1. States Parties shall assure to the child who is capable of forming his or her own views the right to express those views freely in all matters affecting the child, the views of the child being given due weight in accordance with the age and maturity of the child.

2. For this purpose, the child shall in particular be provided the opportunity to be heard in any judicial and administrative proceedings affecting the child, either directly, or through a representative or an appropriate body, in a manner consistent with the procedural rules of national law.

Article 13

1. The child shall have the right to freedom of expression; this right shall include freedom to seek, receive and impart information and ideas of all kinds, regardless of frontiers, either orally, in writing or in print, in the form of art, or through any other media of the child's choice.

2. The exercise of this right may be subject to certain restrictions, but these shall only be such as are provided by law and are necessary:

a) For respect of the rights or reputations of others; or

b) For the protection of national security or of public order (*ordre public*), or of public health or morals.

Article 14

1. States Parties shall respect the right of the child to freedom of thought, conscience and religion.

2. States Parties shall respect the rights and duties of the parents and, when applicable, legal guardians, to provide direction to the child in the exercise of his or her right in a manner consistent with the evolving capacities of the child.

3. Freedom to manifest one's religion or beliefs may be subject only to such limitations as are prescribed by law and are necessary to protect public safety, order, health or morals, or the fundamental rights and freedoms of others.

Article 15

1. States Parties recognize the rights of the child to freedom of association and to freedom of peaceful assembly.

2. No restrictions may be placed on the exercise of these rights other than those imposed in conformity with the law and which are necessary in a democratic society in the interests of national security or public safety, public order (*ordre public*), the protection of public health or morals or the protection of the rights and freedoms of others.

Article 16

1. No child shall be subjected to arbitrary or unlawful interference with his or her privacy, family, home or correspondence, nor to unlawful attacks on his or her honour and reputation.

2. The child has the right to the protection of the law against such inter-ference or attacks.

Article 17

States Parties recognize the important function performed by the mass media and shall ensure that the child has access to information and material from a diversity of national and international sources, especially those aimed at the promotion of his or her social, spiritual and moral well-being and physical and mental health. To this end, States Parties shall:

a) Encourage the mass media to disseminate information and material of social and cultural benefit to the child and in accordance with the spirit of article 29;

b) Encourage international co-operation in the production, exchange and dissemination of such information and material from a diversity of cultural, national and international sources;

c) Encourage the production and dissemination of children's books;

d) Encourage the mass media to have particular regard to the linguistic needs of the child who belongs to a minority group or who is indigenous;

e) Encourage the development of appropriate guidelines for the protection of the child from information and material injurious to his or her well-being, bearing in mind the provisions of articles 13 and 18.

Article 18

1.   States Parties shall use their best efforts to ensure recognition of the principle that both parents have common responsibilities for the upbringing and development of the child. Parents or, as the case may be, legal guardians, have the primary responsibility for the upbringing and development of the child. The best interests of the child will be their basic concern.

2.   For the purpose of guaranteeing and promoting the rights set forth in the present Convention, States Parties shall render appropriate assistance to parents and legal guardians in the performance of their child-rearing responsibilities and shall ensure the development of institutions, facilities and services for the care of children.

3.   States Parties shall take all appropriate measures to ensure that children of working parents have the right to benefit from child-care services and facilities for which they are eligible.

Article 19

1.   States Parties shall take all appropriate legislative, administrative, social and educational measures to protect the child from all forms of physical or mental violence, injury or abuse, neglect or negligent treatment, maltreatment or exploitation, including sexual abuse, while in the care of parent(s), legal guardian(s) or any other person who has the care of the child.

2.   Such protective measures should, as appropriate, include effective procedures for the establishment of social programmes to provide necessary support for the child and for those who have the care of the child, as well as for other forms of prevention and for identification, reporting, referral,

investigation, treatment and follow-up of instances of child maltreatment described heretofore, and, as appropriate, for judicial involvement.

Article 20

1.   A child temporarily or permanently deprived of his or her family environment, or in whose own best interests cannot be allowed to remain in that environment, shall be entitled to special protection and assistance provided by the State.

2.   States Parties shall in accordance with their national laws ensure alternative care for such a child.

3.   Such care could include, *inter alia*, foster placement, Kafala of Islamic law, adoption, or if necessary placement in suitable institutions for the care of children. When considering solutions, due regard shall be paid to the desirability of continuity in a child's upbringing and to the child's ethnic, religious, cultural and linguistic background.

Article 21

States Parties that recognize and/or permit the system of adoption shall ensure that the best interests of the child shall be the paramount consideration and they shall:

a) Ensure that the adoption of a child is authorized only by competent authorities who determine, in accordance with applicable law and procedures and on the basis of all pertinent and reliable information, that the adoption is permissible in view of the child's status concerning parents, relatives and legal guardians and that, if required, the persons concerned have given their informed consent to the adoption on the basis of such counselling as may be necessary;

b) Recognize that intercountry adoption may be considered as an alternative means of child's care, if the child cannot be placed in a foster or an adoptive family or cannot in any suitable manner be cared for in the child's country of origin;

c) Ensure that the child concerned by intercountry adoption enjoys safeguards and standards equivalent to those existing in the case of national adoption;

d) Take all appropriate measures to ensure that, in intercountry adoption, the placement does not result in improper financial gain for those involved in it;

e) Promote, where appropriate, the objectives of the present article by concluding bilateral or multilateral arrangements or agreements, and endeavour, within this framework, to ensure that the placement of the child in another country is carried out by competent authorities or organs.

Article 22

1. States Parties shall take appropriate measures to ensure that a child who is seeking refugee status or who is considered a refugee in accordance with applicable international or domestic law and procedures shall, whether unaccompanied or accompanied by his or her parents or by any other person, receive appropriate protection and humanitarian assistance in the enjoyment of applicable rights set forth in the present Convention and in other international human rights or humanitarian instruments to which the said States are Parties.

2. For this purpose, States Parties shall provide, as they consider appropriate, co-operation in any efforts by the United Nations and other competent intergovernmental organizations or non-governmental organizations co-operating with the United Nations to protect and assist such a child and to trace the parents or other members of the family of any refugee child in order to obtain information necessary for reunification with his or her family. In cases where no parents or other members of the family can be found, the child shall be accorded the same protection as any other child permanently or temporarily deprived of his or her family environment for any reason, as set forth in the present Convention.

Article 23

1. States Parties recognize that a mentally or physically disabled child should enjoy a full and decent life, in conditions which ensure dignity, promote self-reliance, and facilitate the child's active participation in the community.

2. States Parties recognize the right of the disabled child to special care and shall encourage and ensure the extension, subject to available resources, to the eligible child and those responsible for his or her care, of assistance for which application is made and which is appropriate to the child's condition and to the circumstances of the parents or others caring for the child.

3. Recognizing the special needs of a disabled child, assistance extended in accordance with paragraph 2 of the present article shall be provided free of charge, whenever possible, taking into account the financial resources of the parents or others caring for the child, and shall be designed to ensure that the disabled child has effective access to and receives education, training, health care services, rehabilitation services, preparation for employment and recreation opportunities in a manner conducive to the child's achieving the fullest possible social integration and individual development, including his or her cultural and spiritual development.

4. States Parties shall promote, in the spirit of international co-operation, the exchange of appropriate information in the field of preventive health care and of medical, psychological and functional treatment of disabled children, including dissemination of and access to information concerning methods of rehabilitation, education and vocational services, with the aim of enabling States Parties to improve their capabilities and skills and to widen their experience in these areas. In this regard, particular account shall be taken of the needs of developing countries.

Article 24

1. States Parties recognize the right of the child to the enjoyment of the highest attainable standard of health and to facilities for the treatment of illness and rehabilitation of health. States Parties shall strive to ensure that no child is deprived of his or her right of access to such health care services.

2. States Parties shall pursue full implementation of this right and, in particular, shall take appropriate measures:

a) To diminish infant and child mortality;

b) To ensure the provision of necessary medical assistance and health care to all children with emphasis on the development of primary health care;

c) To combat disease and malnutrition including within the framework of primary health care, through *inter alia* the application of readily available technology and through the provision of adequate nutritious foods and clean drinking water, taking into consideration the dangers and risks of environmental pollution;

d) To ensure appropriate pre-natal and post-natal health care for mothers;

e) To ensure that all segments of society, in particular parents and children, are informed, have access to education and are supported in the use of basic knowledge of child health and nutrition, the advantages of breast-feeding, hygiene and environmental sanitation and the prevention of accidents;

f) To develop preventive health care, guidance for parents and family planning education and services.

3. States Parties shall take all effective and appropriate measures with a view to abolishing traditional practices prejudicial to the health of children.

4. States Parties undertake to promote and encourage international co-operation with a view to achieving progressively the full realization of the right recognized in the present article. In this regard, particular account shall be taken of the needs of developing countries.

Article 25

States Parties recognize the right of a child who has been placed by the competent authorities for the purposes of care, protection or treatment of his or her physical or mental health, to a periodic review of the treatment provided to the child and all other circumstances relevant to his or her placement.

Article 26

1. States Parties shall recognize for every child the right to benefit from social security, including social insurance, and shall take the necessary measures to achieve the full realization of this right in accordance with their national law.

2. The benefits should, where appropriate, be granted, taking into account the resources and the circumstances of the child and persons having responsibility for the maintenance of the child, as well as any other consideration relevant to an application for benefits made by or on behalf of the child.

Article 27

1. States Parties recognize the right of every child to a standard of living adequate for the child's physical, mental, spiritual, moral and social development.

2. The parent(s) or others responsible for the child have the primary responsibility to secure, within their abilities and financial capacities, the conditions of living necessary for the child's development.

3. States Parties, in accordance with national conditions and within their means, shall take appropriate measures to assist parents and others responsible for the child to implement this right and shall in case of need provide material assistance and support programmes, particularly with regard to nutrition, clothing and housing.

4. States Parties shall take all appropriate measures to secure the recovery of maintenance for the child from the parents or other persons having financial responsibility for the child, both within the State Party and from abroad. In particular, where the person having financial responsibility for the child lives in a State different from that of the child, States Parties shall promote the accession to international agreements or the conclusion of such agreements, as well as the making of other appropriate arrangements.

Article 28

1. States Parties recognize the right of the child to education, and with a view to achieving this right progressively and on the basis of equal opportunity, they shall, in particular:

a) Make primary education compulsory and available free to all;

b) Encourage the development of different forms of secondary education, including general and vocational education, make them available and accessible to every child, and take appropriate measures such as the introduction of free education and offering financial assistance in case of need;

c) Make higher education accessible to all on the basis of capacity by every appropriate means;

d) Make educational and vocational information and guidance available and accessible to all children;

e) Take measures to encourage regular attendance at schools and the reduction of drop-out rates.

2. States Parties shall take all appropriate measures to ensure that school discipline is administered in a manner consistent with the child's human dignity and in conformity with the present Convention.

3. States Parties shall promote and encourage international co-operation in matters relating to education, in particular with a view to contributing to the elimination of ignorance and illiteracy throughout the world and facilitating access to scientific and technical knowledge and modern teaching methods. In this regard, particular account shall be taken of the needs of developing countries.

Article 29

1. States Parties agree that the education of the child shall be directed to:

a) The development of the child's personality, talents and mental and physical abilities to their fullest potential;

b) The development of respect for human rights and fundamental freedoms, and for the principles enshrined in the Charter of the United Nations;

c) The development of respect for the child's parents, his or her own cultural identity, language and values, for the national values of the country in which the child is living, the country from which he or she may originate, and for civilizations different from his or her own;

d) The preparation of the child for responsible life in a free society, in the spirit of understanding, peace, tolerance, equality of sexes, and friendship among all peoples, ethnic, national and religious groups and persons of indigenous origin;

e) The development of respect for the natural environment.

2. No part of the present article or article 28 shall be construed so as to interfere with the liberty of individuals and bodies to establish and direct educational institutions, subject always to the observance of the principles set forth in paragraph 1 of the present article and to the requirements that the education given in such institutions shall conform to such minimum standards as may be laid down by the State.

Article 30

In those States in which ethnic, religious or linguistic minorities or persons of indigenous origin exist, a child belonging to such a minority or who is indigenous shall not be denied the right, in community with other members of his or her group, to enjoy his or her own culture, to profess and practise his or her own religion, or to use his or her own language.

Article 31

1. States Parties recognize the right of the child to rest and leisure, to engage in play and recreational activities appropriate to the age of the child and to participate freely in cultural life and the arts.

2. States Parties shall respect and promote the right of the child to participate fully in cultural and artistic life and shall encourage the provision of appropriate and equal opportunities for cultural, artistic, recreational and leisure activity.

Article 32

1. States Parties recognize the right of the child to be protected from economic exploitation and from performing any work that is likely to be hazardous or to interfere with the child's education, or to be harmful to the child's health or physical, mental, spiritual, moral or social development.

2. States Parties shall take legislative, administrative, social and educational measures to ensure the implementation of the present article. To this end, and having regard to the relevant provisions of other international instruments, States Parties shall in particular:

a) Provide for a minimum age or minimum ages for admissions to employment;

b) Provide for appropriate regulation of the hours and conditions of employment;

c) Provide for appropriate penalties or other sanctions to ensure the effective enforcement of the present article.

Article 33

States Parties shall take all appropriate measures, including legislative, administrative, social and educational measures, to protect children from the illicit use of narcotic drugs and psychotropic substances as defined in the relevant international treaties, and to prevent the use of children in the illicit production and trafficking of such substances.

Article 34

States Parties undertake to protect the child from all forms of sexual exploitation and sexual abuse. For these purposes, States Parties shall in particular take all appropriate national, bilateral and multilateral measures to prevent:

a) The inducement or coercion of a child to engage in any unlawful sexual activity;

b) The exploitative use of children in prostitution or other unlawful sexual practices;

c) The exploitative use of children in pornographic performances and materials.

Article 35

States Parties shall take all appropriate national, bilateral and multilateral measures to prevent the abduction of, the sale of or traffic in children for any purpose or in any form.

Article 36

States Parties shall protect the child against all other forms of exploitation prejudicial to any aspects of the child's welfare.

Article 37

States Parties shall ensure that:

a) No child shall be subjected to torture or other cruel, inhuman or degrading treatment or punishment. Neither capital punishment nor life imprisonment without possibility of release shall be imposed for offences committed by persons below 18 years of age;

b) No child shall be deprived of his or her liberty unlawfully or arbitrarily. The arrest, detention or imprisonment of a child shall be in conformity with the law and shall be used only as a measure of last resort and for the shortest appropriate period of time;

c) Every child deprived of liberty shall be treated with humanity and respect for the inherent dignity of the human person, and in a manner which takes into account the needs of persons of his or her age. In particular every child deprived of liberty shall be separated from adults unless it is considered in the child's best interest not to do so and shall have the right to maintain contact with his or her family through correspondence and visits, save in exceptional circumstances;

d) Every child deprived of his or her liberty shall have the right to prompt access to legal and other appropriate assistance, as well as the right to challenge the legality of the deprivation of his or her liberty before a court or other competent, independent and impartial authority, and to a prompt decision on any such action.

Article 38

1. States Parties undertake to respect and to ensure respect for rules of international humanitarian law applicable to them in armed conflicts which are relevant to the child.

2. States Parties shall take all feasible measures to ensure that persons who have not attained the age of 15 years do not take a direct part in hostilities.

3. States Parties shall refrain from recruiting any person who has not attained the age of 15 years into their armed forces. In recruiting among those persons who have attained the age of 15 years but who have not attained the age of 18 years, States Parties shall endeavour to give priority to those who are oldest.

4. In accordance with their obligations under international humanitarian law to protect the civilian population in armed conflicts, States Parties shall take all feasible measures to ensure protection and care of children who are affected by an armed conflict.

Article 39

States Parties shall take all appropriate measures to promote physical and psychological recovery and social reintegration of a child victim of: any form of neglect, exploitation, or abuse; torture or any other form of cruel, inhuman or degrading treatment or punishment; or armed conflicts. Such recovery and reintegration shall take place in an environment which fosters the health, self-respect and dignity of the child.

Article 40

1. States Parties recognize the right of every child alleged as, accused of, or recognized as having infringed the penal law to be treated in a manner consistent with the promotion of the child's sense of dignity and worth, which reinforces the child's respect for the human rights and fundamental freedoms of others and which takes into account the child's age and the desirability of promoting the child's reintegration and the child's assuming a constructive role in society.

2. To this end, and having regard to the relevant provisions of international instruments, States Parties shall, in particular, ensure that:

a) No child shall be alleged as, be accused of, or recognized as having infringed the penal law by reason of acts or omissions that were not prohibited by national or international law at the time they were committed;

b) Every child alleged as or accused of having infringed the penal law has at least the following guarantees:

i)   To be presumed innocent until proven guilty according to law;

ii)   To be informed promptly and directly of the charges against him or her, and, if appropriate, through his or her parents or legal guardians, and to have legal or other appropriate assistance in the preparation and presentation of his or her defence;

iii)   To have the matter determined without delay by a competent, independent and impartial authority or judicial body in a fair hearing according to law, in the presence of legal or other appropriate assistance and, unless it is considered not to be in the best interest of the child, in particular, taking into account his or her age or situation, his or her parents or legal guardians;

iv)   Not to be compelled to give testimony or to confess guilt; to examine or have examined adverse witnesses and to obtain the participation and examination of witnesses on his or her behalf under conditions of equality;

v)   If considered to have infringed the penal law, to have this decision and any measures imposed in consequence thereof reviewed by a higher competent, independent and impartial authority or judicial body according to law;

vi)   To have the free assistance of an interpreter if the child cannot understand or speak the language used;

vii)   To have his or her privacy fully respected at all stages of the proceedings.

3.   States Parties shall seek to promote the establishment of laws, procedures, authorities and institutions specifically applicable to children alleged as, accused of, or recognized as having infringed the penal law, and, in particular:

a) the establishment of a minimum age below which children shall be presumed not to have the capacity to infringe the penal law;

b) whenever appropriate and desirable, measures for dealing with such children without resorting to judicial proceedings, providing that human rights and legal safeguards are fully respected.

4. A variety of dispositions, such as care, guidance and supervision orders; counselling; probation; foster care; education and vocational training programmes and other alternatives to institutional care shall be available to ensure that children are dealt with in a manner appropriate to their well-being and proportionate both to their circumstances and the offence.

Article 41

Nothing in the present Convention shall affect any provisions which are more conducive to the realization of the rights of the child and which may be contained in:

a) The law of a State Party; or

b) International law in force for that State.

PART II

Article 42

States Parties undertake to make the principles and provisions of the Convention widely known, by appropriate and active means, to adults and children alike.

Article 43

1. For the purpose of examining the progress made by States Parties in achieving the realization of the obligations undertaken in the present Convention, there shall be established a Committee on the Rights of the Child, which shall carry out the functions hereinafter provided.

2. The Committee shall consist of ten experts of high moral standing and recognized competence in the field covered by this Convention. The members of the Committee shall be elected by States Parties from among their nationals and shall serve in their personal capacity, consideration being given to equitable geographical distribution, as well as to the principal legal systems.

3.   The members of the Committee shall be elected by secret ballot from a list of persons nominated by States Parties. Each State Party may nominate one person from among its own nationals.

4.   The initial election to the Committee shall be held no later than six months after the date of the entry into force of the present Convention and thereafter every second year. At least four months before the date of each election, the Secretary-General of the United Nations shall address a letter to States Parties inviting them to submit their nominations within two months. The Secretary-General shall subsequently prepare a list in alphabetical order of all persons thus nominated, indicating States Parties which have nominated them, and shall submit it to the States Parties to the present Convention.

5.   The elections shall be held at meetings of States Parties convened by the Secretary-General at United Nations Headquarters. At those meetings, for which two thirds of States Parties shall constitute a quorum, the persons elected to the Committee shall be those who obtain the largest number of votes and an absolute majority of the votes of the representatives of States Parties present and voting.

6.   The members of the Committee shall be elected for a term of four years. They shall be eligible for re-election if renominated. The term of five of the members elected at the first election shall expire at the end of two years; immediately after the first election, the names of these five members shall be chosen by lot by the Chairman of the meeting.

7.   If a member of the Committee dies or resigns or declares that for any other cause he or she can no longer perform the duties of the Committee, the State Party which nominated the member shall appoint another expert from among its nationals to serve for the remainder of the term, subject to the approval of the Committee.

8.   The Committee shall establish its own rules of procedure.

9.   The Committee shall elect its officers for a period of two years.

10. The meetings of the Committee shall normally be held at United Nations Headquarters or at any other convenient place as determined by the Committee. The Committee shall normally meet annually. The duration

of the meetings of the Committee shall be determined, and reviewed, if necessary, by a meeting of the States Parties to the present Convention, subject to the approval of the General Assembly.

11. The Secretary-General of the United Nations shall provide the necessary staff and facilities for the effective performance of the functions of the Committee under the present Convention.

12. With the approval of the General Assembly, the members of the Committee established under the present Convention shall receive emoluments from the United Nations resources on such terms and conditions as the Assembly may decide.

Article 44

1. States Parties undertake to submit to the Committee, through the Secretary-General of the United Nations, reports on the measures they have adopted which give effect to the rights recognized herein and on the progress made on the enjoyment of those rights:

a) Within two years of the entry into force of the Convention for the State Party concerned,

b) Thereafter every five years.

2. Reports made under the present article shall indicate factors and difficulties, if any, affecting the degree of fulfilment of the obligations under the present Convention. Reports shall also contain sufficient information to provide the Committee with a comprehensive understanding of the implementation of the Convention in the country concerned.

3. A State Party which has submitted a comprehensive initial report to the Committee need not in its subsequent reports submitted in accordance with paragraph 1(b) of the present article repeat basic information previously provided.

4. The Committee may request from States Parties further information relevant to the implementation of the Convention.

5. The Committee shall submit to the General Assembly, through the Economic and Social Council, every two years, reports on its activities.

6.   States Parties shall make their reports widely available to the public in their own countries.

Article 45

In order to foster the effective implementation of the Convention and to encourage international co-operation in the field covered by the Convention:

a) The specialized agencies, the United Nations Children's Fund and other United Nations organs shall be entitled to be represented at the consideration of the implementation of such provisions of the present Convention as fall within the scope of their mandate. The Committee may invite the specialized agencies, the United Nations Children's Fund and other competent bodies as it may consider appropriate to provide expert advice on the implementation of the Convention in areas falling within the scope of their respective mandates. The Committee may invite the specialized agencies, the United Nations Children's Fund and other United Nations organs to submit reports on the implementation of the Convention in areas falling within the scope of their activities;

b) The Committee shall transmit, as it may consider appropriate, to the specialized agencies, the United Nations Children's Fund and other competent bodies, any reports from States Parties that contain a request, or indicate a need, for technical advice or assistance, along with the Committee's observations and suggestions, if any, on these requests or indications;

c) The Committee may recommend to the General Assembly to request the Secretary-General to undertake on its behalf studies on specific issues relating to the rights of the child;

d) The Committee may make suggestions and general recommendations based on information received pursuant to articles 44 and 45 of the present Convention. Such suggestions and general recommendations shall be transmitted to any State Party concerned and reported to the General Assembly, together with comments, if any, from States Parties.

Part III

Article 46

The present Convention shall be open for signature by all States.

Article 47

The present Convention is subject to ratification. Instruments of ratification shall be deposited with the Secretary-General of the United Nations.

Article 48

The present Convention shall remain open for accession by any State. The instruments of accession shall be deposited with the Secretary-General of the United Nations.

Article 49

1. The present Convention shall enter into force on the thirtieth day following the date of deposit with the Secretary-General of the United Nations of the twentieth instrument of ratification or accession.

2. For each State ratifying or acceding to the Convention after the deposit of the twentieth instrument of ratification or accession, the Convention shall enter into force on the thirtieth day after the deposit by such State of its instrument of ratification or accession.

Article 50

1. Any State Party may propose an amendment and file it with the Secretary-General of the United Nations. The Secretary-General shall thereupon communicate the proposed amendment to States Parties, with a request that they indicate whether they favour a conference of States Parties for the purpose of considering and voting upon the proposals. In the event that, within four months from the date of such communication, at least one third of the States Parties favour such a conference, the Secretary-General shall convene the conference under the auspices of the United Nations.

Any amendment adopted by a majority of States Parties present and voting at the conference shall be submitted to the General Assembly for approval.

2.   An amendment adopted in accordance with paragraph 1 of the present article shall enter into force when it has been approved by the General Assembly of the United Nations and accepted by a two-thirds majority of States Parties.

3.   When an amendment enters into force, it shall be binding on those States Parties which have accepted it, other States Parties still being bound by the provisions of the present Convention and any earlier amendments which they have accepted.

Article 51

1.   The Secretary-General of the United Nations shall receive and circulate to all States the text of reservations made by States at the time of ratification or accession.

2.   A reservation incompatible with the object and purpose of the present Convention shall not be permitted.

3.   Reservations may be withdrawn at any time by notification to that effect addressed to the Secretary-General of the United Nations, who shall then inform all States. Such notification shall take effect on the date on which it is received by the Secretary-General.

Article 52

A State Party may denounce the present Convention by written notification to the Secretary-General of the United Nations. Denunciation becomes effective one year after the date of receipt of the notification by the Secretary-General.

Article 53

The Secretary-General of the United Nations is designated as the depositary of the present Convention.

Article 54

The original of the present Convention, of which the Arabic, Chinese, English, French, Russian and Spanish texts are equally authentic, shall be deposited with the Secretary-General of the United Nations.

In witness thereof the undersigned plenipotentiaries, being duly authorized thereto by their respective Governments, have signed the present Convention.

Other Council of Europe Publishing texts:

Children and adolescents – Protection under the European Social Charter, "Social Charter Monographs", No. 3 (to be published).

The Council of Europe and child welfare. The need for a European convention on children's rights, "Human Rights Files", No. 10, 1989.

Emergency measures in family matters (Recommendation No. R (91) 9), "Legal issues", 1993.

Explanatory report on the European Convention on the Adoption of Children, "Treaties and Reports", No. 58, 1969.

Explanatory report on the European Convention on the Legal Status of Children Born out of Wedlock, "Treaties and Reports", No. 85, 1975.

Explanatory report on the European Convention on Recognition and Enforcement of Decisions concerning Custody of Children and on Restoration of Custody of Children, "Treaties and Reports", No. 105, 1980.

The family, "Social Charter Monographs", No.1, 1995.

Report on the integration of disabled children into their family and society (Steering Committee on Social Policy (CDPS), 1989.

The rights of children – a European perspective, 1996.

Sexual exploitation, pornography, and prostitution of, and trafficking in, children and young adults (Recommendation No. R (91) 11) and report of the European Committee on Crime Problems, "Legal Issues", 1993.

Social reactions to juvenile delinquency (Recommendation No. R. (87) 20); Social reactions to juvenile delinquency among young people coming from migrant families (Recommendation No. R (88) 6), 1989.

Street children, 1994.

Violence in the family (Recommendation No. R (85) 4), "Legal issues",1986.

Young adult offenders and crime policy, "Criminological Research" Vol. XXX, 1994.

In the same series

Mediterranean strategies (1995)
ISBN 92-871-2667-4

Bridging the gap: the social aspects of the new democracies (1995)
ISBN 92-871-2739-5

The gender perspective (1995)
ISBN 92-871-2822-7

Asylum (1995)
ISBN 92-871-2902-9

Sales agents for publications of the Council of Europe
Agents de vente des publications du Conseil de l'Europe

AUSTRALIA/AUSTRALIE
Hunter publications, 58A, Gipps Street
AUS-3066 COLLINGWOOD, Victoria
Fax: (61) 34 19 71 54

AUSTRIA/AUTRICHE
Gerold und Co., Graben 31
A-1011 WIEN 1
Fax: (43) 1512 47 31 29

BELGIUM/BELGIQUE
La Librairie européenne SA
50, avenue A. Jonnart
B-1200 BRUXELLES 20
Fax: (32) 27 35 08 60

Jean de Lannoy
202, avenue du Roi
B-1060 BRUXELLES
Fax: (32) 25 38 08 41

CANADA
Renouf Publishing Company Limited
1294 Algoma Road
CDN-OTTAWA ONT K1B 3W8
Fax: (1) 613 741 54 39

DENMARK/DANEMARK
Munksgaard
PO Box 2148
DK-1016 KØBENHAVN K
Fax: (45) 33 12 93 87

FINLAND/FINLANDE
Akateeminen Kirjakauppa
Keskuskatu 1, PO Box 218
SF-00381 HELSINKI
Fax: (358) 01 21 44 35

GERMANY/ALLEMAGNE
UNO Verlag
Poppelsdorfer Allee 55
D-53115 BONN
Fax: (49) 228 21 74 92

GREECE/GRÈCE
Librairie Kauffmann
Mavrokordatou 9, GR-ATHINAI 106 78
Fax: (30) 13 83 03 20

HUNGARY/HONGRIE
Euro Info Service
Magyarország
Margitsziget (Európa Ház),
H-1138 BUDAPEST
Fax: (36) 1 111 62 16

IRELAND/IRLANDE
Government Stationery Office
4-5 Harcourt Road, IRL-DUBLIN 2
Fax: (353) 14 75 27 60

ISRAEL/ISRAËL
ROY International
PO Box 13056
IL-61130 TEL AVIV
Fax: (972) 3 546 1442

ITALY/ITALIE
Libreria Commissionaria Sansoni
Via Duca di Calabria, 1/1
Casella Postale 552, I-50125 FIRENZE
Fax: (39) 55 64 12 57

MALTA/MALTE
L. Sapienza & Sons Ltd
26 Republic Street
PO Box 36
VALLETTA CMR 01
Fax: (356) 246 182

NETHERLANDS/PAYS-BAS
InOr-publikaties, PO Box 202
NL-7480 AE HAAKSBERGEN
Fax: (31) 542 72 92 96

NORWAY/NORVÈGE
Akademika, A/S Universitetsbokhandel
PO Box 84, Blindern
N-0314 OSLO
Fax: (47) 22 85 30 53

PORTUGAL
Livraria Portugal, Rua do Carmo, 70
P-1200 LISBOA
Fax: (351) 13 47 02 64

SPAIN/ESPAGNE
Mundi-Prensa Libros SA
Castelló 37, E-28001 MADRID
Fax: (34) 15 75 39 98

Llibreria de la Generalitat
Rambla dels Estudis, 118
E-08002 BARCELONA
Fax: (34) 34 12 18 54

SWEDEN/SUÈDE
Aktiebolaget CE Fritzes
Regeringsgatan 12, Box 163 56
S-10327 STOCKHOLM
Fax: (46) 821 43 83

SWITZERLAND/SUISSE
Buchhandlung Heinimann & Co.
Kirchgasse 17, CH-8001 ZÜRICH
Fax: (41) 12 51 14 81

BERSY
Route du Manège 60, CP 4040
CH-1950 SION 4
Fax: (41) 27 31 73 32

TURKEY/TURQUIE
Yab-Yay Yayimcilik Sanayi Dagitim Tic Ltd
Barbaros Bulvari 61 Kat 3 Daire 3
Besiktas, TR-ISTANBUL

UNITED KINGDOM/ROYAUME-UNI
HMSO, Agency Section
51 Nine Elms Lane
GB-LONDON SW8 5DR
Fax: (44) 171 873 82 00

**UNITED STATES and CANADA/
ÉTATS-UNIS et CANADA**
Manhattan Publishing Company
468 Albany Post Road
PO Box 850
CROTON-ON-HUDSON, NY 10520, USA
Fax: (1) 914 271 58 56

———

STRASBOURG
Librairie Kléber
Palais de l'Europe
F-67075 Strasbourg Cedex
Fax: (33) 88 52 91 21

Council of Europe Publishing/Editions du Conseil de l'Europe
Council of Europe/Conseil de l'Europe
F-67075 Strasbourg Cedex
Tel. (33) 88 41 25 81 - Fax (33) 88 41 27 80